DOCTOR SCRATCH

Borgo Press Books by Frank J. Morlock

Castor and Pollux and Other Opera Libretti (Editor)
The Chevalier d'Éon and Other Short Farces (Editor)
Chuzzlewit
Congreve's Comedy of Manners
Crime and Punishment
Cyrano and Molière: Five Plays by or About Molière (Editor)
Doctor Scratch and Other Plays (Editor)
Falstaff (with Shakespeare, John Dennis, & William Kendrick)
Fathers and Sons
Herculaneum & Sardanapalus: Two Opera Libretti (Editor)
The Idiot
Isle of Slaves and Other Plays (Editor)
Jurgen
Justine
The Londoners & The Green Carnation: Two Plays
Lord Jim
The Madwoman of Beresina & Other Napoleonic Plays (Ed.)
Notes from the Underground
Oblomov
Old Creole Days
Outrageous Women: Lady Macbeth and Other Plays (Editor)
Peter and Alexis
The Princess Casamassima
A Raw Youth
Salammbô & Dido: Two Operas (Editor)
The Stendhal Hamlet Scenarios and Other Shakespearean Shorts from the French (Editor)
Two Voltairean Plays: The Triumvirate; Comedy at Ferney
Whitewashing Julia and Other Plays
The Widow's Husband; and, Porthos in Search of an Outfit: Two Dumasian Comedies (Editor)
Zeneida & The Follies of Love & The Cat Who Changed into a Woman: Two Plays (Editor)

DOCTOR SCRATCH AND OTHER PLAYS

FRANK J. MORLOCK,

EDITOR

THE BORGO PRESS
MMXIII

DOCTOR SCRATCH AND OTHER PLAYS

Copyright © 1986, 2013 by Frank J. Morlock

FIRST EDITION

Published by Wildside Press LLC

www.wildsidebooks.com

DEDICATION

To my good friend, Rick Roberts

CONTENTS

DOCTOR SCRATCH, by Noël Le Breton.........9
CAST OF CHARACTERS...................10
ACT I................................11
ACT II...............................32
ACT III..............................63
THE SERVANT PROBLEM, by Alain-René Lesage...91
CAST OF CHARACTERS...................92
THE PLAY.............................93
THE FORFEITURE, by Charles Dufresny.......163
CAST OF CHARACTERS..................164
THE PLAY............................165
ABOUT THE EDITOR....................206

DOCTOR SCRATCH
A COMEDY BY NOËL LE BRETON, SIEUR DE HAUTEROCHE

CAST OF CHARACTERS

Loveless

Gerald

Dr. Bloodgood

Augusta

Olivia

Lettice

Martin

Peg

Scalpel

Big Tom

Scratch

Seven men, four women

ACT I

The scene is London, around 1675. The street before Bloodgood's surgery.

Martin

What, sir? You say you wish to remarry?

Loveless

Yes, yes—I wish to remarry, and to better succeed, I have sent my son to Oxford under the pretext of studying for his degree.

Martin

I understand perfectly. But, may one ask the name of your bride-to-be?

Loveless

Certainly. It's Olivia.

Martin

What! The daughter of Dr. Bloodgood?

Loveless

The same.

Martin

You are joking, sir—this girl isn't yet eighteen, and would be more suitable for your son than for you.

Loveless

I don't intend to let my son marry for three or four years.

Martin

But, sir, did you consider carefully what you are doing when you got this idea to marry Olivia?

Loveless

Did I consider carefully? Yes, yes—I gave it a lot of thought. She's beautiful; she's intelligent; she's young; she's idealistic. In fact, she has a lot of qualities that are simply not to be disparaged.

Martin

Well, these are beautiful traits to keep you from thinking—for to be honest with you, none of these traits go with an old man.

Loveless

Huh? I am not that old!

Martin

Oh, yeah! If we were in those times when men lived seven or eight hundred years—you'd only be an adolescent; but, in the times we live, you're well along in your race.

Loveless

But, sixty years—

Martin

My word. Not to lie, I believe you have at least twelve or fourteen more years, for I remember that the other day the good Mr. Hurtle, drinking a cup of wine with you, said he was more than sixty-six, and that you were in college when he was in first form, and in a college play, he played cupid, and you played King Arthur.

Loveless

He doesn't know what he's talking about; he's one of those men who like to pretend they're older than they are.

Martin

Leave the age business aside, for, as they say, it's only for the grey hair. But, let us talk a little about your marriage. Do you believe that Dr. Bloodgood and Augusta, his wife, will give you their daughter—she being an only child? When one has only a daughter, and marries her—it's in the hope she'll produce grandchildren. But, not to sugar the pill, if you marry her, they run the risk of never having that joy—at least without some assistance—you understand me.

Loveless

None of this is your affair—and I know what I am doing. When she is my wife, we'll do what needs to be done.

Martin

My word, I doubt she ever will be your wife.

Loveless

Well, as for me, I am certain of it. Dr. Bloodgood is a man of his word—he has given me his solemn promise that she will be mine.

Martin

Well, that's something. But, you know that Augusta is a domineering woman—and, if I don't deceive myself, she has the look of wearing the pants.

Loveless

I know she's a little proud. But the advantages I will bring her daughter will soften her pride—and besides, a husband is always the master of his wife.

Martin

Always! My word. I've seen many that don't live agreeably, and who wish with all their heart that you speak true. But, here is Dr. Bloodgood, who is leaving his house.

(Enter Dr. Bloodgood from his house.)

Bloodgood

Ah, it's you, Mr. Loveless?

Loveless

At your service. I came to speak of this business.

Bloodgood

What business?

Loveless

Oh, the one that—you know about it—

Bloodgood

What?

Loveless

The business we spoke about together?

Bloodgood

When?

Loveless

Huh—several times.

Bloodgood

Where?

Loveless

Several places.

Bloodgood

I don't know what it is.

Loveless

About your daughter's marrying me.

Bloodgood

Oh, is that all? I thought you meant something else. About that? You know I've given my word. You've only to choose the day. Rest at ease. You are the master of that business.

Loveless

I'm obligated to you. But, have you taken the trouble to speak to your better half?

Bloodgood

No, but I give you her consent. She's submissive to my will—and I know how to deal with her if she makes any difficulty: I am a man who knows how to inject a little reason into a woman.

Loveless

I don't doubt it.

Bloodgood

Actually, I'd like to see her puff up in front of me. If she crossed me, I would make her see how stupid she is. But, thank heaven, I don't have to trouble. In a word, my wife does everything that I wish.

Loveless

Decide, if you please, which of us will speak of it first to her; it's a propriety I ought to observe, for, as you know, the ladies are jealous of their littler prerogatives.

Bloodgood

Willingly, and to get on with it, I am going to bring her here.

(Exit Dr. Bloodgood into the house.)

Loveless

Well, Martin? What do you say to that?

Martin

Everything's going fine, and I'm very easy because of your father-in-law.

(Enter Dr. Bloodgood with Augusta.)

Bloodgood

Wife, here's our good friend, Mr. Loveless.

Augusta

Ah, I am his servant, and delighted to see him.

Bloodgood (low to Loveless)

It will be more becoming if you speak first.

Loveless (low to Bloodgood)

You begin, then I'll follow up.

Bloodgood (low)

You can explain better than I.

Loveless

Not at all. Besides, reason dictates that you should open the subject.

Bloodgood

It's up to you to take the first step.

Loveless

I've done it for you, and you ought to predispose her before I speak to her.

Augusta

At least, tell me what you're squabbling over, and why you brought me here.

Loveless

A mere bagatelle.

Bloodgood

Wife, it's our friend Mr. Loveless who asks for the hand of our daughter in marriage.

Augusta

And for whom?

Loveless

For me, madam, but under conditions which cannot be disagreeable to you. Doubtless, at first blush, my age would give you some repugnance to the idea—but, when you know, madam, that I will make you a fine settlement on your daughter, and that I will take her without a dowry—and that your husband has already given me his word—I dare to hope you will be as kind.

Augusta

All these matters are very weighty—but your age, sir, does not agree with my daughter's, and one often sees young women who make such marriages fall into disorderly conduct. The caresses of an old man are not meant for a young woman: in fact, they create an antipathy, and we see even nature itself revolt. Thus, to avoid these possible disgraces to my family, you will appreciate why I refuse to give my consent.

Loveless

But, your husband has given me his word.

Augusta

I believe it, but obviously he hasn't considered it carefully, for if he had, he would be—doubtless—of my opinion.

Loveless

Sir, you know you promised me.

Augusta

I believe, as I said before, that he did promise Olivia to you—but he can de-promise her to you—for believe me, it won't happen.

Loveless

Sir, a man of honor ought to hold to his word. Didn't you promise your daughter in marriage to me?

Bloodgood

Hey—all that is true—

Augusta

Well—if he promised her—I did not. And that's enough.

Bloodgood

Wife.

Augusta

Hey—my God, leave me alone. I know very well what I'm doing.

Bloodgood

But, it's necessary—to keep one's—

Augusta

It's necessary not to make such glib promises. One more time, it's never going to happen. And, your arguments couldn't be worse than they are. Goodbye, sir. Get it in your head that you will never marry my daughter.

(Exit)

Augusta

Sir?

Bloodgood

What do you want?

Martin

She's submissive to my will—and I know how to deal with her if she makes any difficulty: I am a man who knows how to inject a little sense into a woman. I'd like to see her puff up in front of me. If she crosses me, I'd make her see how stupid she is. In a word, my wife does everything I wish.

Bloodgood

You are an impertinent!

Loveless

Indeed, Martin's right. And, this is the speech you made to me before we spoke to your wife.

Bloodgood

True, but we must be patient. It's not necessary to get carried away right from the start. Sometimes one ought to temporize. I promised you— All right, leave it to me.

Martin

All right, leave it to him. He'll spoil everything. My word, you'd better believe the words of the wife, and not those of this gentleman. You can see quite clearly that she is the sole mistress and master.

Bloodgood

You don't know what you are saying.

Martin

No, but I know you will be furiously repulsed in any siege effort. Tell me, if you please, who is the boss—you or your wife?

Bloodgood

I am.

Martin

Oh, yeah! In words, but not in deeds.

Bloodgood

You'll learn that I am master in fact, and in words, too. You are a fool!

Martin

Ah, sir, I'm not going to dispute that quality with you.

Bloodgood

Shut up! (to Loveless) Sir, once more—enough— Goodbye.

(Exit Bloodgood into the house.)

Martin

Ho, devilishly well said. Sir, you ought no longer to hope to marry Miss Olivia, because that opinionated and imperious mother will never give her to you. As for the husband, he's a fine doctor, a good astrologer, a great psychic—but he's not master in his own house. You cannot build on his promises.

Loveless

But, don't I see Scratch?

Martin

Yes, sir. It's Scratch, all right.

(Enter Scratch.)

Scratch

Ah! Sir, your servant. Good day, Martin.

Martin

Good day.

Loveless

What brings you to town?

Scratch

Your son sent me by coach. I've only been in town a few hours.

Martin

By coach? You should have been sent on foot.

Loveless

Why did he send you?

Scratch

Sir, here's a letter that will tell you everything.

Loveless (reading)

"Father"—hmm— This isn't his style or handwriting. Are you making fun of me?

Scratch

No, sir. I ask your pardon. You see, I lost his letter on the way. So, I had a peasant who could write make me another one. I know that he was asking for money, and that he promised to be a good boy in the future, and not to do it again. Read the rest of the letter.

Loveless

Huh— I'm satisfied with what I've read.

Martin

What, did you dictate to the peasant?

Scratch

Yeah, I did. What are you getting at?

Martin (ironically)

Nothing. But, it's well-contrived, ho, ho.

Scratch

You know, you always talk big—but by God, remember—I'm smarter than you.

Martin

Ho, ho—without a doubt.

Scratch

Damn! Would you like a punch? You will see—

Loveless

Will you both shut up!

Scratch

But, sir, he always pretends to know everything, and thinks no one's as smart as he is.

Martin

Oh—I defer to you.

Loveless

One more time—shut up. But, Scratch, you say my son has spent all his money after four months.

Scratch

Yes, sir. If it wasn't true, I wouldn't say it.

Loveless

It's gone awfully fast. But, go get some sleep. I will talk to you about it later. I have some pressing business right now. Come on—follow me, Martin.

(Exit Loveless and Martin.)

Scratch

Hola! He thinks he's the only one who knows anything. Damn, when he takes up that grave attitude, you'd think no one else in the world was as wise as he. He acts like he knows more than anybody.— But, let's go to Loveless's and get some money—of which my master has a great need. The expenditures he makes each day! But, I see him coming. It's not a good idea to tell him I lost his letter—he might abuse me.

(Enter Gerald.)

Gerald

Tell me, what are you doing here?

Scratch

Nothing, sir.

Gerald

What—two days after I left you, you haven't been to my father yet?

Scratch

No, sir, but I met him in the street, and that did our business.

Gerald

How is that?

Scratch

I gave him your letter, and told him your need for money. And that, briefly, is all that's happened.

Gerald

And, what did he say to you?

Scratch

Nothing, except to go home and that he would speak to me later. At the moment, he has some business.

Gerald

Didn't he interrogate you about my behavior?

Scratch

Very little, but I expect he soon will, and that is why I must wait on him.

Gerald

Be careful what you say, at least.

Scratch

Hey, leave it to me. We are not so stupid as we are badly dressed. He believes all my nonsense.

Gerald

Watch out for Martin at all times. As you know, he's got a big mouth.

Scratch

I don't care about him! God, because he knows how to read and write, he imagines that I am not as wise as he. I have a good idea to give him a fat lip.

Gerald

He's with my father?

Scratch

Yes, and wants to argue already. But, we've struck back. Go—rely on me. You know that I am not a mere talker—I get things done that you want done. Where are you coming from?

Gerald

Olivia told me she has something she wants to tell me, and that I would find her about this house.— But, I see her coming.

(Enter Olivia and Lettice from the house.)

Olivia

Gerald, you come too soon. I told you to come later. You're two hours early.

Gerald

You're right, madam, but you know the impatience that routinely torments lovers, and how they believe their pains are eased when they can see the place where they will meet the person they love.

Olivia

Gerald, stop the flattery, because I cannot stay long with you. I am going to pay a visit, and my mother will come to get me. You must know something, though. Your father wants to marry me.

Gerald

My father?

Olivia

Yes, your father—and my father has promised me to him. But my mother, you know, rules the roost, and has strongly rebuffed goodman Loveless. Now, see the mess we are in: for when I told my mother the love I had for you, and got her to be favorable to my wishes, your father wouldn't consent. Without your father's agreement, we can hope for nothing from my mother. Goodbye—I am afraid she's coming right behind me.

(Exit Olivia and Lettice. Lettice and Scratch make exaggerated bows to each other.)

Gerald

What should I do now, Scratch?

Scratch

What crazy logic made the old mercenary amorous at the age of seventy-four? Without a doubt, that's why he sent us to Oxford. But, we've got to prevent him from marrying. And that's done only with money—and then, we'll cut him out of the game. Look at the old gallowsbird: he needs girls of eighteen to cheer him up! He isn't completely disgusting—he digests it well—he just needs a refill.

Gerald

But, what to do, Scratch?

Scratch

Try to speak to her alone—and that will resolve all your affairs. She will give you—many possible ways.

Gerald

Come, I am going to write a letter that you will deliver to Lettice when they come home.

Scratch

But, I ought to go to your father's house.

Gerald

I want you to deliver my letter before going there.

CURTAIN

ACT II

A large room in Bloodgood's house. There are several doors. There is a large table used to conduct autopsies.

Bloodgood

Lettice, Lettice, hey! Lettice?

Lettice

Sir?

Bloodgood

Fix this room up properly. I'm going to have some doctors watch the autopsy I will conduct on the corpse the public executioner is sending me.

Lettice

But, sir, why choose this apartment? In the past, you did it in the other house.

Bloodgood

True, but my wife wants me to use the house in the back so the main house will be free. I find she has an excellent idea.

Lettice

Ah! I don't doubt it.

Bloodgood

Because, where we are, over here, the garden which separates these two houses will hold down the noise the opinionated usually make on such occasions. There's always somebody who doesn't agree with the others, and who remembers an erroneous opinion—and makes more noise than four people put together.

Lettice

True, sir, none of you doctors can agree—your science is very uncertain, and you are the first to be deceived.

Bloodgood

Sometimes that happens, but it's not the fault of medicine itself.

Lettice

If it's not the fault of medicine, then, it's the fault of the doctors.

Bloodgood

That may be true, Lettice, but that's none of your business.

Lettice

No, but I can speak my mind, and if it's not my business today, it will be someday—in spite of me.

Bloodgood

Very good. But, let's change that subject, and think of receiving the cadaver—which should be arriving very soon. Put it in the vault, because I won't begin work until tomorrow. Now, I'm going to visit three or four patients for whom I don't have much hope. (leaving)

Lettice

I will do all that you say.

Bloodgood (returning)

Lettice, if you wished to do all that I say, you could show a little feeling for me, and not be angry.

Lettice

You shouldn't be having such thoughts with as nice a looking wife as you have. It seems to me that it's unreasonable, and you ought to be content with her.

Bloodgood

It's a strange diet that consists of only one food. In the end, it's boring.

Lettice

If you wife had the same ideas, what would you say?

Bloodgood

Oh, it's not the same thing. The pride of a man is to cajole several women; the virtue of a woman is to listen to no man except her husband.

Lettice

I don't believe in men having more privileges than women—and what men permit themselves to do, they dare not forbid their wives.

Bloodgood

The law intends that it be this way.

Lettice

In fact, it should be just the opposite. Those who made that law were ignorant—for there are stupid lawyers, just as there are stupid doctors. But, I see clearly—and will guard myself. Go see your patients—and leave me alone!

Bloodgood

No goodbyes, Lettice?

(Exit Bloodgood.)

Lettice

No goodbyes, sir. See this little twerp! Just leave him alone, and he'll do some beautiful things. It's a strange thing when these dogs of men can't content themselves with their wives—they must have some new toy.— If I am ever married, and my husband plays me such tricks—what's sauce for the goose is sauce for the gander.— We'll see! Ah, Scratch, what do you want?

(Enter Scratch.)

Scratch

I was prowling around here to see if I could give you this letter. I saw Dr. Bloodgood leave and I entered, as you see.

Lettice

Close that door, so we can speak securely. I am going to close this one. Well—who sent this letter?

(They each go to a door and close it.)

Scratch

My master. He's becoming desperate because Olivia told him something touching her marriage to his father, Mr. Loveless.

Lettice

We'll have to prevent that—for it shouldn't be.

Scratch

The devil you say. You'd lose more than one person. You'd lose the advantage of having me for a husband—me—who loves you better than fifty could do.

Lettice

You think that's such a great advantage?

Scratch

Undoubtedly. But, let's not speak of that anymore. The gentleman likes the lady and the lady likes the gentleman. Tell me, what were you doing here with Dr. Bloodgood?

Lettice

Getting ready for tomorrow's dissection of a hanged man. And, because he's chosen this place to do it, he ordered me to spruce it up. Now—it's necessary for your master to take special measures to speak to Olivia. Since this place is going to be occupied, they won't have much chance to meet here, as they used to do. Give me the letter; I will give it to Olivia and get a quick reply.

Scratch

Here—go quickly.

Bloodgood (knocking at the other door)

Hey, hey, Lettice—open up for me, I'm in a hurry.

Lettice

My God, what am I going to do? It's our master.

Scratch

Ah, dammit, I wish I were a long way from here.

Augusta (knocking at the other door)

Hey, Lettice—open for me.

Lettice

This is getting worse! That's our mistress.

Scratch

Ah—it's the devil!

Lettice

If she weren't here, I could put you in the vault.

Bloodgood

Come on, open for me, Lettice.

Lettice

I am lost.

Scratch

Me, too.

Lettice

Scratch, lie down in this table. I am going to say you are the cadaver of the hanged man.

Scratch

But—

Lettice

Don't argue—do what I tell you.

(Scratch lies on the table and Lettice opens the door for Dr. Bloodgood.)

Bloodgood (entering quickly)

You are waiting carefully on me! I forgot something around here, and I have got to go find it quickly.

(Exit Bloodgood by a door near the one which Augusta is knocking on. Lettice now opens for Augusta.)

Augusta

Where were you when I was calling you?

Lettice

I was busy receiving the cadaver—and I didn't hear you at first.

(Enter Dr. Bloodgood.)

Bloodgood

Wife—what are you doing here?

Augusta

I came to see if Lettice has got things ready as she was supposed to.

Bloodgood

See you, see you.

(Exit Bloodgood.)

Augusta

Lettice, take care of everything here. As for me, I'm going—

'cause I don't like to look at these things—they always give me gloomy ideas.

(Exit Augusta.)

Lettice

Go, go, madam, I will do all that is necessary. (shutting and locking both doors) Well, Scratch, my trick seems to have worked.

Scratch

Very well—and we got out of it cheaply—but, I must leave soon to avoid new trouble. Perhaps I could remain a little longer, usefully—

Bloodgood (returning)

Lettice, Lettice, open up. It's me.

Lettice

Ah—get back in the same posture: it's our doctor.

Scratch (getting back)

Devil take him.

(Enter Bloodgood.)

Bloodgood

I think I've got a hangover today. I've forgotten half the things I need. Certain pills I need. But, Lettice, what do I see here?

Lettice

It's the cadaver they just brought. It was already here when you came before.

Bloodgood

Very good. But, how come he still has his clothes on?

Lettice

They said they'd come and get them later.

Bloodgood (examining the body)

Nothing missing. I am of the opinion that since the body is still warm, maybe I ought to begin the dissection immediately. Go look for my lancet and scalpel. They're high up in my cabinet.

Lettice

But, sir, you aren't prepared. It would be very difficult, and besides, your patients are waiting for you.

Bloodgood

To wait two or three hours is no big thing.

Lettice

But, suppose they died?

Bloodgood

Not my fault. If they die in such a short time, my visit wouldn't help them much.

Lettice

But, a timely remedy—

Bloodgood

Go and bring me a box of twine and staples; you'll find them with my instruments. While he's still warm, I have a better chance of finding the duct veins and the reservoirs which conduct the chlye to the heart during fibrillation.

Lettice

But sir, you aren't going to take away my privilege to fix this place the way I want. Come tomorrow, as you said.

Bloodgood

Either go, or I will go myself.

Lettice

I will go, if you insist.

(Exit Lettice.)

Bloodgood (looking at the cadaver and addressing it)

He doesn't look evil—yet, there's something about his face. Yes, all the rules of craniotomy and physiognomy are false if this fellow didn't deserve to be hanged. I'll incise him here (pointing) and open him up; from his xyphoid cartilage right down to his pubis. (listening) His heart's still beating. Ah, if I had some of my colleagues here now. Particularly those who don't believe in the circulation of the blood—would I ever show them!

(Enter Scalpel, a surgeon.)

Scalpel

Sir, sir, the squire is very bloated since yesterday. You ought to see him soon.

Bloodgood

I will go soon—but, I haven't the leisure at present.

Scalpel

But, the illness presses, sir— It's necessary that you come now.

Bloodgood

I cannot—go, bleed him, and I will see him in a couple of hours.

Scalpel

Sir, I don't believe that bleeding will do him any good.

Bloodgood

Bleed him, I tell you. I know better what I'm doing.

Scalpel

But, sir—

Bloodgood

But—one more time: bleed him!

Scalpel

But, but, sir—

Bloodgood

See here! I intend that he be bled. What business have surgeons to argue with doctors?

Scalpel

Sir, I won't bleed him anymore. I believe another bleeding is capable of causing his death.

Bloodgood

He's going to be bled whether you like it or not. I will get someone else to do it, if necessary.

Scalpel

Do what you please, but I am not going to do it. Good day!

Bloodgood

Good day!

(Exit surgeon Scalpel to the street. Lettice returns from the house.)

Lettice (having heard)

I don't know how to find your hiding place—and besides, madam has told me you are wanted urgently at the Squire's.

Bloodgood

I'll have to put it off till tomorrow, Lettice. Put this cadaver in the vault.

(Exit Bloodgood.)

Lettice (closing the door after him)

Go. I will manage everything.

Scratch (getting up)

Without amusing myself in a discussion any further, I am going to leave immediately.

Lettice

Where do you intend to go?

Scratch

Devil knows! Where I intend to go? Let me out of here. What! You coolly get the scalpel and other gimcracks to dissect me in small pieces—and, you want me to stay! You're making fun of me.

Lettice

Understand, that when I left to find the equipment, I intended to hide it where he'd never find it. And that's what I did.

Scratch

Ho, that's a good idea. At first I was astonished, me—your future husband—that you had the sangfroid to see me cut up so barbarously.

Lettice

I would never have permitted it. But, pay attention to me. I am going to try to give this letter to Olivia, and get a reply.

Scratch

I don't want to wait here—

Lettice

Why?

Scratch

The word lancet makes me tremble. I am going to wait in the street—there I don't fear the doctor's scalpel. The fear I experienced in this place is more than enough.

Lettice

Go, but don't be impatient.

Scratch

I'll wait forever—when I'm out of here. (as he is leaving, someone knocks at the street door) Ah, the devil again! As soon as you open it, I'm running out.

Lettice

Don't do it, you'll spoil everything. Lie down again, quickly.

Scratch

I won't do it—anything could happen. Suppose he had a scalpel in his pocket?

Lettice

If I hadn't forgotten the key to the vault, I would put you there.

Scratch

Do what you want, but I'm not being put anywhere.

Lettice

Listen, I am going to get you a doctor's robe—you will say that, having learned he was going to do a dissection, you decided to pay him a visit. As for the cadaver, I will say I put it in the vault.

(More knocking. Lettice goes to a closet and returns with a robe.)

Scratch

Go, I prefer to be a doctor to a cadaver. But God, think how I am dressed. At least in these clothes, I run no risk of being split open. If I appear ignorant, there are plenty of other doctors who are more so.

Lettice (returning)

Hurry—put it on so I can open the door.

Scratch

Here I am now.

(Lettice opens. Enter Peg.)

Peg

Is the doctor here?

Lettice

No.

Peg

There he is. Why do you hide him from me? Just let me say a couple of words to him.

Scratch (gravely)

What do you want from me?

Peg

Sir, you know my mistress has lost a little dog that she loves to distraction—and she's very upset and blames it all on me. They tell me you're an astrologer as well as a doctor?

Scratch

I'm as wise in one as the other.

Peg

That's why I came—to beg you to give me some news of this little dog.

Scratch

How long has it been lost?

Peg

Two days.

Scratch

At what time was it lost?

Peg

Eleven in the morning.

Scratch

What color is it?

Peg

Black and white.

Scratch (pondering)

That's all I need to know.

Peg (to Lettice)

Oh, the wonderful man—he's going to give us news of the little dog.

Lettice

Without a doubt.

Scratch

Listen—two days, you say?

Peg

Yes, sir.

Scratch

At eleven o'clock.

Peg

Yes.

Scratch

Black and white?

Peg

Yes.

Scratch

Take some pills.

Peg

Some pills?

Scratch

Yes.

Peg

But will pills find the dog?

Scratch

Yes.

Peg

But, still—what kind of pills?

Scratch

Blue pills. The kind you see at the pharmacy.

Peg

But, sir—

Scratch

I haven't the time to explain. Do exactly as I say.

Peg

How many should I take?

Scratch

Three.

Peg (offering a silver coin)

That's enough. If I find my dog this way, I'm going to send you a lot of customers.

Scratch

If you don't find it, it's not the fault of the pills.

Peg

I believe you. Goodbye, sir.

(Exit Peg.)

Scratch

Goodbye.

Lettice (after having reshut the door)

Well, Scratch, you've hardly put on your white coat when you get your first patient and make your fee.

Scratch

The devil! I can see it's a fine profession. Without knowing what I'm doing, I coin money—and without running the risk of playing cadaver.

Lettice

I could hardly prevent myself from laughing at your prescription. Blue pills for finding a lost dog.

Scratch

What the devil do you want me to prescribe—surgery? I can't read or write and I know nothing of what she was interested in. The idea of pills came to me, so I prescribed them. I'm taking off this costume, so I can wait in the street, as I said.

(More knocking.)

Lettice

They're knocking. Put it back on.

Scratch

Again? I fear it may be the doctor.

Lettice

Who cares? We'll pull the wool over his eyes, too.

(Lettice opens the door. Enter Big Tom.)

Tom

Doctor Bloodgood is home?

Lettice

Why?

Tom

I wish to speak to him.

Lettice

About what?

Tom

Something concerning me.

Lettice

Who are you?

Tom

I am someone you don't know.

Lettice

I know that! Does Dr. Bloodgood know you?

Tom

No, nor I, him.

Scratch (gravely)

What do you wish?

Lettice

This gentleman wishes to speak to you.

Scratch

Let him come in, and be brief.

Tom (after several bows)

People say you're a very good doctor, and also know about divination. So, you see, after I was told this, I decided to speak to you about a little matter.

Scratch

Speak a little more concisely.

Tom

You see, I love a girl in our village, and there's a certain character who visits her, too—I want to know if she loves me like she says, and if I will marry her. For to tell you the truth, I am doubtful.

Scratch

What's she like?

Tom

She's big, dark, and pug-nosed.

Scratch

Big, dark, and pug-nosed?

Tom

Yes, sir.

Scratch

Take some pills.

Tom

Some pills?

Scratch

Yes.

Tom

Some pills—

Scratch

Yes, some pills, green ones, that you can get at the pharmacy. You'll have to take at least ten, on account of your size.

Tom

But, it seems to me that pills are good for illness, not for—

Scratch

Go do what I tell you, and the pills will do the rest. It's a science that few understand. If you were educated, and if you knew Latin, I would explain such things to you.

Tom

Sir, I know Latin, because I'm a judge in our village.

Scratch

You know Latin?

Tom

Yes, sir.

Scratch

Well, so much the better for you. Some other time—now, do what I tell you. Good day. I have other business.

Tom

Before going, I have to pay up.

Scratch

That's a good idea.

Tom (feeling in his pocket)

Some pills—

Scratch (taking him by the arm and escorting him out)

Yes, some pills, yes, some pills, quickly, quickly, and good day.

Tom

Here's a gold piece. If this works—

Scratch

I accept. That's enough for the advice I've given you.

Tom (aside)

These savants are always so brusque! (aloud) Good day, sir.

Scratch

Your servant.

(Exit Big Tom.)

Lettice (having closed the door)

A gold piece and a silver crown, in so little time! Well, you ought to give me half, since I made you a doctor.

Scratch

Lettice, leave me alone. We will feed heartily together—but, for now—

(More knocking.)

Lettice

Someone's knocking again— We're getting lots of experience—

Scratch

By God, I'm getting out of here. Ah, here's the devil again—

(Enter Dr. Bloodgood.)

Bloodgood

Lettice, have you been dreaming?

Lettice

Sir, I just put the cadaver in the vault, and here is one of your colleagues who heard you were making a dissection, and is come to watch you.

Bloodgood (after several bows)

Sir, although I haven't the honor of knowing you—you are always welcome. But, I won't begin to work until tomorrow. If you wish to do me a favor, you could give ear to a little speech I wish to rehearse—I believe it's a bit unusual.

Scratch

Ah, sir! I wouldn't miss it. The reputation of Dr. Bloodgood in these matters—is, in fact, one—that—I wouldn't miss it.

Lettice

Sir, if you want me to fix up this room, then you must give me freedom from all these interruptions.

Bloodgood

Later. Sir, I'd like to ask you some advice about a patient I'm treating.

Scratch

Sir, you'll excuse me, if you please, I have some pressing business.

Bloodgood

I will be brief. You know this patient had a quatrain fever—tertian and continual—and now, we have broken that fever. But, there remains a thing which worries me about him.—For, besides bad insomnia, which tires him out, his sputum is extremely white—and, to my way of thinking, a very bad sign, because as Hypocrites tells us, "a pituita alba, acqua inter cutem supervenit"—. As you know it's what the Greeks call "leucophlegmatia." If, according to Hypocrites, this white sputum is a sign that hydropsy ought to follow—do you think it necessary to prevent this by giving him a more powerful dosage?

Scratch

You hardly need my advice. You are a man who—in fact, I can say not a thing.

Bloodgood

No, speak frankly—I will be very pleased to know your opinion about it.

Scratch

I am far from knowing very—

Bloodgood

As for me, I reason in this manner. I am not one of those physicians who cherish their own opinion, and who, rather than give up their opinion, let a patient die. Speak, I will listen to you.

Lettice (low to Scratch)

Say what you can. (aloud to Bloodgood) Sir, hurry up, I have a lot to do.

Bloodgood

Lettice, another minute, please.

Scratch

Sir, in these cases—I don't know if—about that—

Bloodgood

Hmm?

Scratch

Some pills—

Bloodgood

To give him some pills would ruin his constitution, which is already much altered by his other infirmities.

Scratch

I didn't say that. I said that some pills I took this morning oblige me to leave you instantly.

Bloodgood

Oh, I don't want to contradict you. Lettice, conduct the doctor where he needs to go. I am your servant.

(Exit Bloodgood into the house.)

Lettice

I am going to make haste to get a reply to this letter, and think, so as to manage things so that when the real cadaver is brought in, no one will notice the difference.

Scratch

And, I am going to wait for you elsewhere, without any more discussion.

CURTAIN

ACT III

The street before Bloodgood's surgery.

Scratch

Well, sir, what do you think of my adventure?

Gerald

I say they're unusual.

Scratch

Cadaver, doctor, cords, scalpels, gimcracks, pills—my God, it's too much.

Gerald

True, it was a lot to put up with—but, you've got to go back again.

Scratch

Me, sir?

Gerald

Yes, you yourself.

Scratch

By God, I don't want to go back for an autopsy, or to get beaten up— You could go yourself.

Gerald

It's true that I could—but, I'm afraid if I do, I might ruin my love affair. If Dr. Bloodgood sees me return, he won't fail to advise my father of everything that's happened. As for you— you risk nothing, because he doesn't know you.

Scratch

I hazard my back, my arms, my legs, my beautiful body. From the way I heard Dr. Bloodgood speak of cords and scalpels, a doctor has no more pity on a man than a lawyer.

Gerald

Still, it's necessary, my dear Scratch, to return one more time. And, you may be certain, that when I can, I will remember your good services and repay them.

Scratch

Ah, I don't doubt it—but, at least, tell me the reason I must return.

Gerald

Here! Listen to this letter you brought me. (reading)

"I have many things to tell you, but I haven't the time to write them. To achieve what we wish, it's necessary to employ several stratagems. Send Scratch as soon as possible. I will make every effort to give him a letter which will instruct you. If I can manage to talk with you in person, believe that I will joyfully do so. Goodbye. Love me as I love you, and rest assured that I will never marry anyone else. Olivia." Well, you see, Scratch.

Scratch

Yeah, I see. I've got to go back. But, if Dr. Bloodgood, who has seen me as both a cadaver and as a doctor, should recognize me—how do I get out of it without a beating—hmm?

Gerald

That's certainly rather a poser.— But, my dear Scratch, you must risk something for your master. Think, devise something so you run no risk.

Scratch

Listen—get me a doctor's outfit. I'd rather appear before him in that way than like a cadaver. For the rest, I'll get out of it the best way I can. I was almost caught by the pills. I'll escape by some other remedy.

Gerald

I'll go get the outfit you want. Now, go to my father's to get the money he promised you. Quite possibly, we'll have real need of it.

Scratch

I'm going—but teach me a bit of Latin. How to say, "I am a

doctor."

Gerald

Sure. Medicus Sum.

Scratch

Medicus Sum. Medicus Sum.

Gerald

Very good.

(Exit Gerald.)

Scratch

Enough! Goodbye. Go think about the costume, and I will go to your father. Medicus Sum, Medicus Sum. What a nice thing to know Latin. Have to repeat, so as not to forget. Medicus Sum, Medicus Sum. That's it. Let's go see Mr. Loveless. But, I see him coming.

(Enter Loveless and Martin.)

Loveless

What are you doing in this place?

Scratch

Sir, I got bored at home and took a walk.

Loveless

Where is your master—tell me?

Scratch

What a fine question! He's at Oxford. Will you please give me the money so I can go back?

Loveless

Oh, yeah—tell me—where does he lodge at Oxford?

Scratch

He lodges near the university.

Loveless

What's the name of the street?

Scratch

The street?

Loveless

Yes.

Scratch

Oh—the name—the name— You were there before me, you know it well.

Loveless

But now?

Scratch

It escapes me. There are rascally names in that city which are difficult to retain, and I don't know how to get them into my head. And besides, I don't care. What's the good of fussing about these bastards of names? He stays where he stays.

Martin

He's quite right.

Scratch

Damn—shut up—or, you will see. Now—

Loveless

Patience.

Scratch

What I don't like is for him to mess into something which is none of his business.

Loveless

Shut up! What does your master do most of the time?

Scratch

He studies—he often dines with people who speak Latin like the very devil. That I find funny—cause when they quarrel, it's as if they were strangling, and the whites of their eyes show. Afterwards, they calm down by each drinking five or six draughts.

Loveless

Not a bad story—but now, two or three persons have told me that he is in this city, and that they have seen him.

Scratch

Whoever said that's a liar, and I will defy him before all of England.

Loveless

We're not getting anywhere. Confess the truth. He's here?

Scratch

I don't confess anything, because it isn't true.

Loveless

Oh, I know everything. If you continue to pretend—

Scratch

You want me, then, to say something which isn't true?

Loveless

I've been lied to.

Scratch

Whatever you please, but it isn't true, it isn't.

Martin

Sir, leave this impudent fellow—he'll put you in an unreasoning rage.

Scratch

Impertinent! Damn—you liar—I'm going to let you have a taste of my knuckles.

(Martin and Scratch start to fight.)

Loveless (separating them with his cane)

Rogues, if you do not stop, I will give you a beating. Ah, damn—it's too much. Scratch, if your master isn't in London, I order you to go find him at Oxford, and tell him that when he lets me know his address, I will send him money by a banker in that city.

Scratch

But, sir—

Loveless

Don't talk anymore—don't come near my house if you don't want to get beat up.

Scratch

If you beat me, I don't know what I'll do.

Loveless

What will you do?

Scratch (shoving Martin)

I'll warm him up like the devil.

Loveless

Why did you do that to him?

Scratch

Hey, why do you plan to beat me?

Loveless

Because you're a cheat.

Scratch

Then, because he's a toady, and wants to see me beaten.

Loveless (raising his cane)

I will teach you—

Scratch

Teach—and see if I don't teach you back—

Loveless

Ah, God, I cannot suffer any more of this.

(Loveless attempts to beat Scratch with his cane. Scratch breaks his head and causes Loveless to fall, then Scratch punches Martin and Martin falls on the other side. Exit Scratch.)

Martin

Ah, the traitor. I believe he's crippled me with a single blow.

Loveless

Martin, come help me to get up.

Martin

Hey, sir, I need someone to help me up, myself.

Loveless (getting up, aided by Martin)

The rogue—he will pay.

Martin

When I catch up with him, then he'll repent.

Loveless

I've hurt my shoulder falling.

Martin

And me—I believe my jaw's broken.

Loveless

He gave us a furious blow.

Martin

With all his might.

Loveless

Patience.

Martin

It's necessary to have a rematch: me against him.

Loveless

Go see if Dr. Bloodgood is at home.

Martin

What, sir? You wish to speak to him again about your marriage, after his wife has said "never" to your face?

Loveless

No matter. I wish to try again—tentatively.

Martin

Very good. That's to say, you want to be refused again. And, you enjoy hearing them chant your praises—rubbing your fur the wrong way.

Loveless

I admit to you, frankly, that I expect a refusal. But, I want to have the pleasure of telling Dr. Bloodgood that I will never think of him except as a man who is led around by the nose like a fool. That will console me.

Martin

But, what good will that do?

Loveless

Just do what I say—see if he is at home.

Martin (knocking)

Hallo!

Lettice (opening)

Who is it?

Martin

Is Doctor Bloodgood here?

Lettice

No. Who wants him?

Loveless

Me, my dear.

Lettice

He isn't in. Do you wish to speak to madam? She's upstairs sleeping. I will go wake her.

Loveless

Let her sleep. My dear child, if you could, by your good offices, get her to consent to give me Olivia, I would—

Lettice

Give you Olivia in marriage? What the devil's got into you at your age?

Loveless

Really, I would—

Lettice

My word, whatever you would do would be worthless. But, do you have anything else to say to me? I am going back in the house.

Loveless

My dear, say to Dr. Bloodgood that his friend, Loveless, came to see him—and that I pray he thinks about what he promised me. Good day, child.

(Exit Loveless and Martin. Enter Scratch, as a doctor, from the opposite direction.)

Scratch (talking to someone offstage)

At home, at home, I tell you. I will reply to you in good time.

Lettice (hearing this, awaits Scratch)

What's up, Scratch—and how'd you get rigged up like this?

Scratch

I saw two people who told me they were studying medicine and asked me advice about the—the—transconfusion of the blood. They insisted I speak. Almost had to be rude to get away from them.

Lettice

What did they tell you?

Scratch

How the devil do I know. Arteries—littoral blood—arterial— An escalation where the blood comes in— Something about an anima—animal who doesn't know any better. The bad blood flowing back. The good in the veins of some other animal. Now, devil take them with all their arguments.

Lettice

You ought to prescribe pills.

Scratch

I would have, with all my heart, but they each had fifty in their pockets.

Lettice (laughing)

But, why are you like this?

Scratch

To have easier access to your home, and to—

(Enter Loveless and Martin.)

Loveless (returning)

My dear Lettice, I had forgotten to give you this ring, but I wish to—

(Scratch turns aside.)

Martin

Sir, if I'm not deceived, that's Scratch, dressed as a doctor.

Loveless

What the devil are you doing here in that outfit?

Scratch (gravely)

What do you want from me? Have you some secret illness? Speak; in the absence of Dr. Bloodgood, I can give you some good advice.

Loveless

No, rogue—we are not ill.

Scratch

Rogue!

Loveless

Yes, rogue.

Scratch

Non sum rogus. Medicus Sum. Medicus Sum.

Loveless

You—a doctor!

Scratch

Yes, doctor—and you are an impertinent. ABACA, LOSTVOI, BARITONAVII, PORLUTOM, Transconfusion. If you were sane, I would speak to you about transconfusion and arterial. But, I can see what your problem is. Go—take some pills.

Loveless

If I take a stick, I'll give you a terrible beating.

Lettice

Sir, come in and wait for our master inside. Leave these extravagants—.

Scratch (entering the house with Lettice)

You're right. That's a better idea.

(Exit Lettice and Scratch into the house.)

Martin

Sir, I question whether that's Scratch. 'Cause he speaks Latin.

Loveless

Rest assured, it's him—and I think there must be some trick up. I want to go in and find out what it is. (knocking at the door)

(Enter Lettice.)

Lettice

What do you want, sir? Do you want to quarrel with that honest man who is in our home?

Loveless

He's a cheating valet.

Lettice

That's untrue—he's one of our master's colleagues. And you have a bad grace to speak of him in that way. I will complain about all of this as soon as—

(Enter Dr. Bloodgood.)

Bloodgood (speaking offstage)

I tell you that this is not possible, and you entertain a wild opinion—

Loveless

Sir—

Bloodgood

You'd have to think a long time to imagine a thing so far from common sense.

Loveless

Sir, I wish—

Bloodgood

Without a doubt, that visionary idea comes from a man with a fever—a very hot fever.

Lettice

What's the matter with you, sir, that you carry on this way with yourself?

Bloodgood

Some people have an opinion about transfusion which is so absurd, so—

Lettice

They're crazy—

Bloodgood

Without a doubt.

Loveless

They're not unreasonable, because it's been publicly condemned, you know.

(Enter Peg.)

Peg (to Lettice)

Dr. Bloodgood's here?

Lettice

There he is. Just in time.

Bloodgood

What do you want?

Peg

I want you hanged! You prescribed pills that almost killed me.

Bloodgood

Me?

Peg

You, you. Deceivers like you. You prescribe things that are wrong and not indicated. Go—take them, and see what happens to you. Pills for finding a lost dog!

Bloodgood

You're mistaken, I've never seen you.

Peg

Never! Didn't I just give you a silver crown?

Bloodgood

You're crazy.

Peg

You're lying and—

(Enter Big Tom.)

Tom

Ah, if I meet this Dr. Bloodgood, I am going to expose his racket—

Peg

Hold—there he is.

Tom

By God, sir, you must be a complete fool to prescribe pills to find out if a woman likes you. And, I was fool enough to take them. They almost sent me to the next world—and I haven't yet returned.

Bloodgood

You're both crazy to speak to me like that. I don't know you.

Tom

Didn't I just give you a golden crown?

Peg

He'll deny everything—just like he did with me.

Bloodgood

You should be put in Bedlam—both of you— You're mad.

Tom

Damn! You're lying—I am not crazy. Peace on this nonsense, or I will give you a taste of my stick on your ears.

Peg

And I—I will pull out your hair.

Bloodgood

This is too much to bear. Lettice, go find a constable.

Tom

Let her go, let her go. I will wait for him.

Peg

And me, too.

Tom

You see how these doctors kill people—and they're always so plausible. By Jove, I want my gold crown back.

Lettice

My word, if you don't be quiet, I am going for the constable.

Tom

That's what I want.

Peg

And that's what I'm waiting for.

(Enter Augusta and Scratch from the house.)

Scratch

But, madam—

Augusta

Once more, sir. I don't want my daughter speaking to men tête-à-tête. If you wish to see my husband, you can return when he's at home.

Scratch

Madam, can you believe that—

Augusta

I know what I believe. Once again—you can't come in when my husband is not home.

Peg (to Big Tom)

It seems to me that face strongly resembles that of the doctor who prescribed pills for me.

Tom

By Jove, it's the doctor who tried to kill me. Ah, deceiver—you will give me back my money.

Peg

Mine, too. (taking Scratch by the collar) Ah, rogue! I've got you now.

Scratch

Non sum rogus. Medicus Sum.

Bloodgood

Good people, you shouldn't maltreat a doctor like that—at least let him explain his reasons.

Loveless

He's the valet of my son.

Peg

He's the doctor who prescribed pills for us.

Tom

And who has given me an awful pain.

Loveless

Rogue! Reply to all these charges.

Scratch

Sir, I can't pretend anymore. Your son never left London, because of the love he had for Miss Olivia Bloodgood. She loves him passionately—and they love each other. And, they coerced me and several other people to serve them in their intrigues.

Augusta

My daughter loves your master?

Scratch

Yes, madam, and powerfully.

Augusta

As for the son—perhaps—but the father must never hope to marry Olivia.

Tom

But, why did you tell us to take pills? How could that advance the intrigues of your master?

Scratch

Those are matters which I will explain at another time.

Bloodgood

You see how you blamed me without cause? Be good enough to come back another time and I promise to satisfy you in one way or another.

Peg

I agree. But, don't fail.

Tom

I agree, too. But no more pills, if you please.

Bloodgood

No. Good day.

(Exit Big Tom and Peg.)

Loveless

You say your master is deeply in love with Olivia?

Scratch

Yes, sir. And a hundred times more than I told you.

Loveless

Well—in that case, I can see I'll have to let him marry her—providing the mother and father consent also.

Bloodgood

For me—I wish it with all my heart—providing, of course, my wife wishes it.

Augusta

I don't really know if I should—

Bloodgood

But, wifey—

Augusta

Since you beg me, I will agree.

Loveless

Where's your master now?

Scratch

I see him coming. Just in time.

(Enter Gerald.)

Loveless

Welcome, gentleman from Oxford.

Gerald (hurling himself at his father's knees)

Ah, daddy—I ask your forgiveness.

Bloodgood

Hey, my God—let's leave this discussion. Let's go inside and talk it all over at leisure.

Augusta

Good idea. Come, go in.

Bloodgood

Go in, Mr. Loveless. The honor is yours.

Loveless

As you please—let's go in.

Scratch

Martin.

Martin

What do you want?

Scratch

Since all I did was crowned with success, by Jove, I'm going in, too.

They all enter the Doctor's house as the

CURTAIN FALLS

THE SERVANT PROBLEM
BY ALAIN-RENÉ LESAGE

CAST OF CHARACTERS

Mr. Touchwood

Mrs. Touchwood

Angelica

Worthy

Mr. Richly

Lucy

Bendish

Bellamy

Five men, three women

THE PLAY

The street before Mr. Touchwood's house.

Worthy

Ah, there you are, jackass!

Bendish

Let's speak without intruding personalities!

Worthy

You scoundrel!

Bendish

Let's leave our attributes out of this sort. I beg you, what are you complaining about?

Worthy

What am I complaining about, Judas! You asked me for eight days' leave, and I haven't seen you for a month. Is that a way for a valet to behave?

Bendish

I beg your pardon, sir, but I serve you in the same manner as you pay me. No pay, no work. We neither have much to complain about.

Worthy

I'd like to know what you've been doing.

Bendish

I've been making my fortune.

Worthy

How's that?

Bendish

By levying a tax on those who are not skilled at poker.

Worthy

Well, you're just in time. I'm out of money and I propose to draw on your exchequer.

Bendish

Sorry, sir: we didn't have a good catch. Too many fish saw the hook.

Worthy

Never mind, Bendish. I'll forgive you. I need your help.

Bendish

How fine of you, sir.

Worthy

I'm in a scrape.

Bendish

Your creditors are after you?

Worthy

No.

Bendish

Oh, I see. The generous person of quality that cosigned your tailor's bill has discovered that we padded it?

Worthy

It's not that either. I've fallen in love!

Bendish

Oh, no! Who is it, by the way?

Worthy

Angelica.

Bendish

Oh, I know the lady. Has a rich father—

Worthy

Well-to-do. He owns three mansions.

Bendish

The adorable Angelica!

Worthy

And, he's got a lot of ready money.

Bendish

Ah, now I understand the extent of your passion! But, are you in with her? Does she know how much you want her?

Worthy

I've had free access to her the last eight days, and I've done my business so well that she looks on me favorably—but Lucy, her maid, told me something yesterday that has upset me completely.

Bendish

Eh? What has this upsetting little Lucy told you?

Worthy

That I have a rival. That her father has given his word to marry her to some provincial hick who may arrive at almost any moment.

Bendish

And, who is this rival?

Worthy

That's what I don't know yet. Lucy was called away just as she was about to tell me, and I was obliged to leave without learning his name.

Bendish

Well—it looks as though we won't be the lucky owners of three stately mansions.

Worthy

Go find Lucy and talk to her for me. Find out. After that, we will make our plans.

Bendish

Leave it to me.

Worthy

I'll wait for you. (exits)

Bendish (to himself)

That I am stationed in life as a valet! Well, it's my own fault. I'm too frivolous—still, I'd be a brilliant financier. I'd have gone bankrupt at least once.

(Enter Bellamy.)

Bellamy

Isn't that Bendish?

Bendish

Isn't that Bellamy?

Bellamy

It is Bellamy, or I'm a goner.

Bendish

What a lucky meeting. Let me hug you, my friend. You know, not seeing you for so long, I was afraid something had happened to you.

Bellamy

I've been in jail.

Bendish

What! What did you do?

Bellamy

One night, I was civil enough to ask a foreigner on the street for news of his own country. He didn't speak a word of English and thought I was trying to rob him. He yelled thief, and I was arrested.

Bendish

For how long?

Bellamy

Seven months. I'd be there still if it hadn't been for the niece of a laundress.

Bendish

Really?

Bellamy

They were terribly prejudiced against me. But the laundress was the mistress of a judge, and so my innocence was demonstrated.

Bendish

It's nice to have powerful friends.

Bellamy

This little adventure has given me a lot to think about.

Bendish

I believe you. You're no longer curious about foreign countries?

Bellamy

Not in the least. Content to stay at home forever. Anyway, I'm back in service. And, what are you doing?

Bendish

I'm an honorary criminal, like you. I work in the service of a gentleman of no means who supposes that a valet works for love, not wages. I'm not too happy with my condition.

Bellamy

Mine is all right. I work for a hick called Richly. He's a likable young kid: he loves gambling, drinking, and fast women. An accomplished gentleman. He's saved me from a life of crime.

Bendish

Innocent life!

Bellamy

Really.

Bendish

Quite. But tell me, Bellamy, why've you come to London? Where are you going?

Bellamy

I'm going into that house.

Bendish

The Touchwood mansion?

Bellamy

His daughter's engaged to Richly.

Bendish

Angelica is betrothed to your master?

Bellamy

His father and Angelica's father are old buddies. And they arranged this marriage to suit themselves.

Bendish

It's all concluded?

Bellamy

Signed and sealed. The dowry is twenty thousand pounds in ready money. They're just waiting for Richly to come so they can settle up.

Bellamy

Well, that being the case, my master, Worthy, had better seek his fortune elsewhere.

Bellamy

What? Your master?

Bendish

He is in love with the same Angelica—while Richly—

Bellamy

Don't worry, Richly isn't going to marry Angelica. There's a minor difficulty.

Bendish

Heh! What?

Bellamy

While his father was busy marrying him, he was busy marrying himself.

Bendish

How did it happen?

Bellamy

He loves a lady who has bestowed so many favors on him that she's in a delicate condition. Richly has to marry her.

Bendish

Well, it's a whole new ball game.

Bellamy

I've been sent to straighten things out and explain everything.

Bendish

Explain everything?

Bellamy

That's what brings me here. Old man Richly is ashamed to do it himself. Afraid they'll be mad. So he sent me. No goodbyes, Bendish. We'll see each other again.

Bendish

Wait, Bellamy, wait, my boy. I've just had an idea. Tell me, is your master known to Angelica's father?

Bellamy

They've never met.

Bendish

Wow! If you're willing, there's a beautiful job to be done. But, after your spell in jail, you probably lack the nerve?

Bellamy

No, no. Me lack nerve! Never. I used to be scared of prison. Not anymore. You behold a finished gentleman, Bendish. I suppose you want your master to impersonate Richly and marry the lady?

Bendish

My master? Think again! He would be a pleasant booby for a girl like Angelica. I destine her for someone better—

Bellamy

Who might that be?

Bendish

Myself, of course.

Bellamy

Well, to say the least, you've got brass.

Bendish

I'm also in love with her.

Bellamy

I bless you both.

Bendish

I will take the name Richly. I will marry Angelica.

Bellamy

If you're asking my consent, I'll give it.

Bendish

I will take the dowry.

Bellamy

Better still.

Bendish

And I will vanish before it comes to an explanation.

Bellamy

Repeat that?

Bendish

Why?

Bellamy

You speak of vanishing with the dowry. That plan needs a small, but important correction.

Bendish

I don't see why.

Bellamy

It makes no mention of me.

Bendish

Oh! WE will vanish with the dowry. Together, my boy.

Bellamy

Oh, on that condition, I am your willing accomplice. But, where will we hide the dowry?

Bendish

In a land, far, far away.

Bellamy

The best place in the world. When do we start?

Bendish

We'll see. Tell me about Angelica's father.

Bellamy

A merchant, pure and simple. A little on the testy side.

Bendish

And his wife?

Bellamy

Still in her teens, although close to sixty—vain, and very changeable.

Bendish

Enough! All that is necessary is to—

Bellamy

Adopt the manners and clothes of my master. You know, you're really almost the same figure.

Bendish

Hum! Then, you say he's good-looking?

Bellamy

Someone's coming out. Now, that's my cue to go in, and put our plans in effect.

Bendish

While you're doing that, I'll neutralize Worthy by persuading him to stay away from Angelica for a few days.

(Exit Bellamy to the house and Bendish in another direction. Enter Angelica and Lucy.)

Angelica

Oh, Lucy, since Worthy has disclosed his passion to me, I feel, I feel, as if—I feel as if—I feel if I marry Richly, I'll never be happy in my life.

Lucy

Worthy is a dangerous man.

Angelica

Woe is me. Help me, Lucy. What should I do? Tell me, I beg you.

Lucy

What advice can I give you?

Angelica

The kind of advice that comes from the interest you take in everything I do.

Lucy

There are only two kinds of advice I can give you. One, forget Worthy. Two, rebel against your father. You're too much in love to forget Worthy, and I really can't counsel you to rebel against your father when I take his money. It's a wash, as you see.

Angelica

Oh, Lucy, you break my heart.

Lucy

Wait! Maybe there's some advice I can give you that will help you, and won't burden my conscience. I have it. Let's find your mother.

Angelica

But, what will we say to her?

Lucy

Tell her everything. Pour your heart out to her. She likes to be flattered and stroked. Flatter and stroke her. She cares for you as much as a vain thing like that can care for anyone—and she will force your papa to withdraw his promise.

Angelica

You're right, Lucy, but I'm afraid.

Lucy

Why?

Angelica

You know my mother. Her spirit is in a perpetual ferment.

Lucy

It's true, she's always of the opinion of the person who spoke to her last. Never mind. We can't afford not to make her an ally. But, I see her coming. Hide for a minute, and come back when I give you the high sign.

(Exit Angelica.)

Lucy

To be sure, Mrs. Touchwood is one of the kindest ladies in England.

Mrs. Touchwood (entering)

You're a flatterer, Lucy.

Lucy

Oh, Madame, I didn't see you! What a fright you gave me! What you overheard was the end of a conversation I was having with your daughter. I was explaining to her about this marriage. I told her that her mother is the most reasonable of mothers.

Mrs. Touchwood

You're right. I'm not like most women. I'm always dispassionate.

Lucy

Without a doubt.

Mrs. Touchwood

I don't let myself get carried away.

Lucy

Absolutely. The most understanding mother in the world. If your daughter didn't want to marry this Richly, I know you wouldn't force her.

Mrs. Touchwood

Me! Force her? Me, torture my daughter? Never. May God forbid I should ever do that to my daughter. Tell me, Lucy, does she dislike Mr. Richly?

Lucy

Oh, but—

Mrs. Touchwood

Don't hide anything from me.

Lucy

Since I can't keep things from you, Madame—yes—she abhors the marriage.

Mrs. Touchwood

And perhaps, she loves another?

Lucy

You've got it.

Mrs. Touchwood

Just like me! I would never have married her father if my colonel hadn't met an untimely death. Who is the gallant young soldier who has won her heart?

Lucy

The young boy who's been coming around lately.

Mrs. Touchwood

Who? Worthy?

Lucy

The same.

Mrs. Touchwood

That reminds me. He looked at Angelica and me yesterday with such pleading eyes. Are you sure it's my daughter he's in love with?

Lucy (signing to Angelica)

Oh, yes, Madame, he told me so himself.

Mrs. Touchwood

Well, if it's really true—

Angelica (entering hastily)

Forgive me, mother, if my feelings aren't as you would wish, but you see—

Mrs. Touchwood

I know it's impossible for a young girl to control her feelings. I know how difficult it is. I sympathize. In a word, we must get Mr. Worthy for you.

Angelica

I can't tell you how much I owe your kindness.

Lucy

It's not enough, Madame. Mr. Touchwood is a trifle opinionated. If you don't—

Mrs. Touchwood

Oh, don't worry. I can manage your father. Just watch me.

(Enter Mr. Touchwood.)

Mrs. Touchwood

You've come just in time, my dear; I have to tell you that I am no longer part of your scheme to force Angelica to marry Richly.

Mr. Touchwood

Ah! Ah! May one ask, my dear, why you've changed your mind?

Mrs. Touchwood

I've found a better husband for her. Worthy wants her. True, he isn't as well off as Richly, but he's a gentleman—and, and, we ought to overlook his poverty because of his very fine blue blood.

Lucy

Wonderful!

Mr. Touchwood

I think very highly of Mr. Worthy. I would willingly give him to Angelica, without regard to his comparative poverty, if I could do so honorably—but it can't be done, my dear.

Mrs. Touchwood

Why not, I'd like to know?

Mr. Touchwood

Why not? Do you want us to break our word to our dear old friend Richly? You don't dislike him for some reason, do you?

Mrs. Touchwood

No.

Lucy

Courage. Don't weaken.

Mr. Touchwood

Well, if you don't dislike him, how can you think of putting such an affront on him? Remember, the agreement is signed and sealed, the invitations have been sent out, and we are only awaiting the arrival of the groom. The whole thing is too far advanced now to break it off, or so it seems to me.

Mrs. Touchwood

I didn't think of all that.

Lucy

Goodbye. The weathercock turns.

Mr. Touchwood

You're too reasonable, my dear, to wish to break off this

marriage.

Mrs. Touchwood

Who said anything about breaking it off? Out of the question!

Lucy

She's killing me! Isn't she a woman? Isn't she a woman? Why can't she be unreasonable and contradict everything?

Mrs. Touchwood

You see, Lucy, I've done everything I can for Worthy.

Lucy

Indeed. A whole lot of good.

Mr. Touchwood

I see young Richly's valet coming.

(Enter Bellamy.)

Bellamy

Your very humble servant, sir and Madame. And to you, Miss Angelica. Hi, Lucy.

Mr. Touchwood

Well, Bellamy, what's the latest news?

Bellamy

Mr. Richly, your son-in-law and my master, has just come from Oxford. He's right behind me, so to speak, and I am come to prepare you.

Angelica

Oh, heavens!

Mr. Touchwood

I can't wait to see him. But, he didn't need to send you—he should have come along himself. On the terms we are, he shouldn't be so formal.

Bellamy

Oh, sir, he's a real gentleman, with exquisite manners. I say it, even though I am his valet—there isn't another gentleman like him in the entire kingdom.

Mrs. Touchwood

Is he smooth? Is he well-educated?

Bellamy

Oh, completely, Madame. He was raised with the best of the nobility. My God! He's extremely sensitive.

Mr. Touchwood

And, his father isn't with him?

Bellamy

No, sir. A bad case of the gout prevents his coming.

Mr. Touchwood

The poor gentleman.

Bellamy

Here's a letter he wrote you.

Mr. Touchwood (reading)

"To Dr. Croaker at Gravesend—"

Bellamy

Oh, that's not it, sir.

Mr. Touchwood

Brr! I wouldn't want to be his patient.

Bellamy (pulling out several letters)

I've got several letters to deliver. Let's see here. "To lawyers Lawless and Crookshank in Gallows Road." That's not it either. "To Messers Gourmand, Pudding Lane." Damn it! I will never find it, I think. Ah, "to Mr. Touchwood." Here it is.

Mr. Touchwood

Hard to read.

Bellamy

He wrote it in a hand trembling with gout. You probably won't recognize the handwriting.

Mr. Touchwood

No, it doesn't look like his handwriting at all. Poor fellow.

Bellamy

Gout is a terrible disease. Heaven preserve us from it.

Mr. Touchwood (reading)

"I wanted to come but the gout prevents me. However, a father needn't be present at a wedding and I don't want the wedding delayed because of my illness. Above all things, it will be a comfort in my old age. I send you my son—be a father to him, and give him away properly. I know you will know how to do it. Your affectionate friend, Richly." It makes me feel for him. But who is this young man coming? Can it be young Richly?

Bellamy

It's himself. What do you think, Madame? Doesn't he have an ingratiating bearing?

Mrs. Touchwood

He's not bad-looking—that's a fact.

(Enter Bendish.)

Bendish

Bellamy.

Bellamy

Sir?

Bendish

Is this Mr. Touchwood, my illustrious father-in-law?

Bellamy

Yes. You've got the original before you.

Mr. Touchwood

Welcome, son-in-law. Give me a hug.

Bendish

My joy is too great to express. (to Mrs. Touchwood) No doubt, this is the child I am to marry?

Mr. Touchwood

No, no, my boy. That's my wife. Here's my daughter, Angelica.

Bendish

Damn it all! What a gorgeous family. I'd willingly marry one and make my mistress of the other.

Mrs. Touchwood

Oooh! What a gallant gentleman. (to Lucy) He appears to have you-know-what, Lucy.

Lucy

And good taste, too, Madame.

Bendish

What an air, what grace, what noble pride. Madame, you are adorable. My father told me: you will see in Mrs. Touchwood a most striking beauty.

Mrs. Touchwood

Get away with you!

Bendish

He said, "I wish she were a widow. I'd be remarried in a minute."

Mrs. Touchwood

Well, I am—! Much obliged.

Mr. Touchwood

I really value your father tremendously, and I'm quite put out he couldn't come with you.

Bendish

It kills him not to be at the wedding. He had promised himself a dance with your darling wife.

Bellamy

He begs you to celebrate the wedding without delay because he is furiously impatient to have it done.

Mr. Touchwood

Everything's ready. All we have to do is pay the dowry.

Bendish

Pay the dowry? Oh, that's a good idea. Let me give Bellamy some instructions. Go to the Marquis— (low) Get the horses ready, tonight, understand? (aloud) —and tell him I kiss his hands.

Bellamy (exiting)

I fly.

Mr. Touchwood

Getting back to your father. I'm very sorry about his indisposition. But I wish you'd satisfy my curiosity—give me some news of his lawsuit.

Bendish

Bellamy—

Mr. Touchwood

You seem troubled—something wrong?

Bendish

Out of the question. I have forgotten to instruct Bellamy. (low) He should have told me about the lawsuit.

Mr. Touchwood

He'll be back. Well now, about the case—has it gone to trial?

Bendish

Yes, thank God, it's over.

Mr. Touchwood

And, did you win?

Bendish

With interest.

Mr. Touchwood

I'm delighted, I assure you.

Bendish

My father took it to heart. It almost drove him crazy.

Mr. Touchwood

My word, it must have cost him a lot of money.

Bendish

But justice cannot be bought.

Mr. Touchwood

I agree. I meant the litigation must have been costly, troublesome.

Bendish

You can't conceive. He was tied up with the most unreasonable man.

Mr. Touchwood

Men? I thought his adversary was a woman?

Bendish

Yes—it was a woman. Right. But, the woman had a certain old Scotsman who advised her. This old man caused my father all sorts of trouble. But, let's talk of something else. I prefer to talk of the wedding, and the pleasure of seeing your wife.

Mr. Touchwood

Well, let's go, my boy. Come on in. I am going to send for the minister.

Bendish (giving Mrs. Touchwood his hand)

Madame.

Mrs. Touchwood (to Angelica)

You have nothing to complain of, my dear. Richly is a very worthy, delightful young man.

(Exit Bendish, Mr. Touchwood, and Mrs. Touchwood into the

house.)

Angelica

Oh, lord, what's going to become of me?

Lucy

You're going to become Mrs. Richly—that's not hard to figure out.

Angelica (crying)

Oh, Lucy. You know how I feel. Show me that you care.

Lucy (crying)

Poor child.

Angelica

Are you so hard-hearted as to leave me to my fate?

Lucy

You break my heart.

Angelica

Lucy, my dear Lucy.

Lucy

Say no more. I am so touched, that I'm going to give you some bad advice—and you're just crazy enough to take it.

Worthy (returning, low)

Bendish told me not to put in an appearance here for several days—because he's got a plan—but he didn't explain it to me. I can't live with this kind of tension.

Lucy

Worthy's coming.

Worthy (low)

No—I'm not just deceiving myself. It's Angelica. Beautiful Angelica. (aloud) Tell me my fate. What will happen? But what, you're both in tears.

Lucy

Oh, yes, sir. We are both in tears—we have no hope—your rival has come.

Worthy

What do I hear?

Lucy

And, he marries my lady tonight.

Worthy

Just heaven.

Lucy

At least, after the marriage, she'll live in London for a while.

You can sometimes get together.

Worthy

I'll die. But Lucy, who is this rival who has taken from me all I care about in this life?

Lucy

His name is Richly.

Worthy

Richly.

Lucy

He's from Oxford.

Worthy

I know everybody from there, and the only Richly I know is the son of Squire Richly.

Lucy

Exactly. The son of Squire Richly is your rival.

Worthy

Oh, if we have only that Richly to fear, there's nothing to worry about.

Angelica

What do you say, Mr. Worthy?

Worthy

Let's stop tormenting ourselves, charming Angelica. Young Richly has been married for at least a week.

Lucy (whistling)

Whew!

Angelica

Don't jest, Worthy. Richly is here, ready to receive my hand.

Lucy

He's this very minute closeted with Ma and Pa.

Worthy

Richly is one of my friends—and he wrote Ma a week ago. I have his letter at home.

Angelica

What did he tell you?

Worthy

That he secretly married a lady of quality.

Lucy

Married secretly. Let us announce this little affair. It should be worth the trouble. Go, sir. Go fetch the letter, and don't waste a minute.

Worthy (exiting)

I'll be back immediately.

Lucy

And, as for us—let's not neglect to make use of this news. I'll be very surprised if we can't make good use of it. It ought, at least, to delay your marriage. I see your father coming. Run to your mother, and tell her while I work on your father.

(Exit Angelica. Enter Mr. Touchwood.)

Mr. Touchwood

Worthy just left you, Lucy?

Lucy

Yes, sir. He just told us something which I swear will surprise you.

Mr. Touchwood

And, what might that be?

Lucy

My word! Richly is a nice fellow, to want two wives, while some honest men have trouble getting one.

Mr. Touchwood

What are you talking about?

Lucy

Richly is married. He has secretly married a lady of quality.

Mr. Touchwood

Good. And, that's all, Lucy?

Lucy

Nothing is more true, sir. Richly himself has written about it to Mr. Worthy, who is his friend.

Mr. Touchwood

You are telling me a big fib. And, I tell you—

Lucy

No, sir, I assure you. Worthy has gone to fetch the letter—it only remains for you to see it.

Mr. Touchwood

Another put-up job. I cannot credit what you say.

Lucy

Eh, sir, why don't you believe it? Aren't people capable of almost anything these days?

Mr. Touchwood

It's true, the world's more corrupt than it was in my day—

Lucy

How do you know this Richly isn't the type of scoundrel who doesn't mind collecting more than one dowry? Now, the wife he has already married, being a woman of rank—this may have results not altogether agreeable to you.

Mr. Touchwood

What you say makes a bit of sense, and is worthy of careful consideration.

Lucy

Huh—careful thought! If I were in your place, before I'd deliver up my girl, the least I'd do is insist on an explanation.

Mr. Touchwood

Right. I see Richly's valet coming. I must sound him to the depths. Withdraw, Lucy, and leave me alone with him.

Lucy

If only this news can be confirmed.

(Exit Lucy. Enter Bellamy.)

Mr. Touchwood

Come here, Bellamy, come on. I find you have the look of an honest man.

Bellamy

Oh, sir, in all modesty, I'm even more honest than I look.

Mr. Touchwood

I'm sure of it. Listen, your master has the bearing of a true gallant.

Bellamy

By Jove, he's a fine fellow. The women are mad about him. He has a certain freedom in his bearing that charms them. By marrying him, his father assures the tranquility of at least thirty households.

Mr. Touchwood

In that case, it doesn't surprise me that he's taken in a certain lady of quality.

Bellamy

What are you talking about, sir?

Mr. Touchwood

It's necessary, my friend, for you to tell me the truth. I know everything. I know that Richly is married.

Bellamy

Ouf!

Mr. Touchwood

You look upset. I see I was told the truth. You are a swindler, too.

Bellamy

I, sir?

Mr. Touchwood

Yes, you—gallows-bird! Your whole plan has been discovered to me, and I am going to have you punished as an accomplice to a criminal plan.

Bellamy

What criminal plan? May I die if I know what you are talking about.

Mr. Touchwood

Go ahead, feign innocence, blockhead—but if you don't quickly confess everything to me, I'm going to have the law on you!

Bellamy

Do what you please, sir. I have nothing to confess to you. I don't know what your complaint is against me.

Mr. Touchwood

You won't talk, eh? Hey, someone—fetch a policeman.

Bellamy

Wait, sir—no need for a lot of trouble. Innocent, though I am, you are taking a tone which makes it hard for me to prove it. Calmly, now. Who told you my master is married?

Mr. Touchwood

Who? He has written so himself, to his friend, Worthy.

Bellamy

To Worthy, you say?

Mr. Touchwood

To Worthy. What do you say to that?

Bellamy

Nothing. God, it's an excellent trick. So, Mr. Worthy, your trick takes.

Mr. Touchwood

What—what do you mean?

Bellamy

They told us that sooner or later, we'd be faced with something like this.

Mr. Touchwood

I don't see your point.

Bellamy

You're going to see it, you're going to see it. First of all, this Mr. Worthy loves your daughter. I will lay a bet.

Mr. Touchwood

I am well aware of that.

Bellamy

Lucy is in his interests. She is in all his plans. I am going to venture, she is the one who told you that lie?

Mr. Touchwood

She told me, yes.

Bellamy

In the debacle caused by the arrival of my master, what could they do? Simple. They say Mr. Richly is married. Worthy himself presents the supposed letter that he says he received from my master—and only to prevent or delay the marriage.

Mr. Touchwood

What you say is very plausible.

Bellamy

And, while you are engaged in this brouhaha, Lucy fortifies the spirit of her mistress—and will make her do something wild—after which you will HAVE TO marry her to Mr. Worthy.

Mr. Touchwood

Whew! It's likely enough to happen as you say.

Bellamy

But, by Jove, the deceivers are deceived. Mr. Touchwood is a man who can think, and knows how to play their games.

Mr. Touchwood

Right, right.

Bellamy

You know all these tricks that a lover employs to beat his rivals out.

Mr. Touchwood

And, I say—I can see quite plainly it's a trick. Let's admire Worthy's trick. He says he's an intimate friend of Richly's—and I'm going to bet they don't even know each other.

Bellamy

Without a doubt! Whew! Sir, you are insightful. Nothing escapes you.

Mr. Touchwood

I'm seldom deceived in my deductions. I see your master coming. I want to joke with him over his supposed marriage. Ha, ha, ha.

Bellamy

Ha, ha, ha—hee, hee, hee.

(Enter Bendish.)

Mr. Touchwood

You'll never guess, son-in-law, what they're saying of you. Oh, is it funny! They warn me—warn me, as if it were a certainty—that you are married. They say you've secretly married a woman from Oxford. Ha, ha, ha—don't you find that funny?

Bellamy (making signs to Bendish)

Really, that's hilarious, ha, ha, ha.

Mr. Touchwood

Somebody else would be stupid enough to believe it. Not me!

Bellamy

Mr. Touchwood is so deep.

Bendish

I would like to know who the author is of such a ridiculous slander!

Bellamy

Mr. Touchwood says it's a gentleman called Worthy.

Bendish

Worth—who is he?

Bellamy (low to Touchwood)

You see, sir, he doesn't know him. (aloud to Bendish) He's your intimate friend, right?

Bendish

Oh, I know who he is. He's my rival. He ought to give up, but he prefers to dream on of sleeping with your daughter. His creditors ardently wish him married.

Mr. Touchwood

They'll have to wait, truly, they'll have to wait.

Bellamy

He isn't stupid, this Worthy, he isn't stupid.

Mr. Touchwood

And I am not dumb either. No, by Jove, I'm not. And to show him, I'm going right now to my attorney. But, before I go—I promised your father to give you twenty thousand pounds cash—but if you like, I'll give you instead a house I own on this very street worth thirty thousand.

Bendish

I'm always a sharp bargainer—but in this case, I prefer the cash.

Bellamy

Money's portable.

Mr. Touchwood

As you like.

Bendish

Yes. It's easier to put in a bag. I want to buy some land in Oxford.

Bellamy

If it's the property I'm thinking about, you'll love it there.

Bendish

I can buy it for fifteen and in five years, I'll sell it for forty.

Bellamy

At least, at least. Hmm. Without speaking of the rest, it has two lakes from which they take out a big catch of fish.

Mr. Touchwood

Well, don't let such a good thing go by. Listen, I have fifty thousand pounds I've been saving to buy a country estate from a nabob who's recently gone bankrupt. Let me give you that to invest—

Bendish

What beneficence! I'll never forget you. My heart will forever— I can't express my gratitude.

Bellamy

Mr. Touchwood is a paragon of fathers-in-law.

Mr. Touchwood

I am going to fetch this money. But, before I go, I must have a word with my wife.

Bendish

Worthy's creditors can go hang.

Mr. Touchwood

Yes, let them hang. I want you to marry Angelica within the hour.

Bendish

Ah, what a joke that will be.

Bellamy

Yes, it will be very funny.

(Exit Touchwood.)

Bendish

Apparently, my master has had an explanation with Angelica and he knows Worthy.

Bellamy

So well that they write to each other, as you see. But, thanks to my efforts, Mr. Touchwood is prejudiced against Worthy, and I hope we can get our hands on the dowry before he is disabused.

Bendish

Oh, heaven.

Bellamy

What's wrong, Bendish?

Bendish

My master is coming here.

Bellamy

Goddamn rotten luck—infuriating.

(Enter Worthy, at a distance, with a letter in his hand.)

Worthy

I'm going to take this letter to Mr. Touchwood. (seeing Bendish, but not recognizing him) But, I see a man. Is it Richly? Wait a minute— I'd better be sure. Heavens! It's Bendish.

Bendish

It's me. What the devil are you doing here? Didn't I forbid you to come to this house? You're going to ruin everything I've accomplished for you.

Worthy

It's no longer necessary to employ any stratagem for me, my dear Bendish.

Bendish

Why?

Worthy

I know the name of my rival. He's called Richly. I have nothing to fear from him. He's married.

Bendish

Richly is married? (showing Bellamy) Wait a sec, sir—here's his valet, whom I've enlisted in your cause. He is going to tell you some news.

Worthy

Is it possible that Richly has written me something untrue? But, why would he write me in these terms? (reading)

"You know, my dear friend, I was married here in Oxford a few days ago. I secretly married a lady of quality. Soon, I am coming to London, where I intend to give you a viva voce account. Richly."

Bellamy

Ah, sir, now I understand. When my master wrote you this letter, he regarded himself as almost married—you understand he had received the last favor from the lady—but Old Richly, instead of approving the match, prevented it.

Worthy

Richly really isn't married?

Bellamy

Right!

Bendish

He isn't married.

Worthy

My dear friends, I beg your help. Bendish, what plan have you formed? I see you don't want to tell me yet. But, don't leave me in all this anxiety. I can't bear it. Why this disguise? What do you plan to do for me?

Bendish

Your friend and rival is not yet in London. In fact, he won't get here for two days. In the mean time, I plan to make Mr. Touchwood rue the day he ever made this engagement.

Worthy

How?

Bendish

By pretending to be Richly. I've already behaved like a perfect idiot. I talk and act foolishly. Both mother and father are disgusted. You know what Mrs. Touchwood is like—she eats up flattery. Well, I've said some things to her that wouldn't flatter a whale.

Worthy

Really?

Bendish

Really. I do and say all kinds of stupid things—and if all goes well, they'll soon throw me out, and marry Angelica to you.

Worthy

And Lucy, is she in it, too?

Bendish

Yes, sir—she's making music with us.

Worthy

Oh, Bendish, I owe you everything.

Bendish (showing Bellamy)

Ask this fellow here, if I'm playing my part to the hilt?

Bellamy

Oh, sir, you've got one smart valet. He's the biggest cheat in London. He orchestrates the whole thing. But, truthfully, I don't play a bad second. If our little game succeeds you'll owe it as much to me as to him.

Worthy

You can both count on my remembering this—I promise you.

Bendish

Never mind the promise. I know you'll never forget us. But think that, if you are seen with us, all will be lost. Get out of here, and don't come back today.

Worthy

I'm going. Goodbye, my friends. I rest in your hands.

Bendish

Rest easy, sir. Now, leave quickly. Leave your fate to us.

Worthy

Remember that—my fate—

Bendish

No more talk.

Worthy

—depends on you.

Bendish (pushing him off)

Get out of here, right now.

(Exit Worthy.)

Bellamy

Finally, he's gone.

Bendish

I can breathe again.

Bellamy

We've had a narrow escape. I would have died if Mr. Touchwood had surprised us with your master.

Bendish

Me, too. But, now we have nothing to fear. We can be certain of success. Now, as to the escape route. Have you secured the horses?

Bellamy

Yes.

Bendish

Great! I suggest we take the Dover road.

Bellamy (distracted)

The Dover road. Very good. Well thought out. My idea exactly.

Bendish

What are you looking at with so much concentration?

Bellamy

I am looking—yes—no—hell and damnation—is it him?

Bendish

Is it who?

Bellamy

Uh-oh—it looks exactly like him.

Bendish

Like who?

Bellamy

Bendish, my poor Bendish—it's old man Richly.

Bendish

Richly's father?

Bellamy

Himself.

Bendish

Cursed old man.

Bellamy

I believe that all the devils in hell are against us.

Bendish

He's coming here. If he gets into Touchwood's house, the game is over.

Bellamy

We've got to prevent him if possible. Go wait in the park. Now what I fear most is that Touchwood may put in an appearance while I'm bamboozling Richly.

(Enter Richly.)

Richly

I don't know what kind of reception I'm going to get from Mr. and Mrs. Touchwood.

Bellamy

You aren't yet there. Your servant, Mr. Richly.

Richly

Oh, I didn't see you, Bellamy.

Bellamy

Well, this is a surprise. What are you doing in London?

Richly

I left Oxford a little after you, because, after thinking about it, it seemed better that I speak for myself. It's pretty shameful to withdraw my solemn word through the mouth of a valet.

Bellamy

I see you really have a delicate sense of honor. And so, you intend to deliver this message to Mr. and Mrs. Touchwood?

Richly

That's my intention.

Bellamy

Thank heaven for sending me here in time to prevent you from doing it.

Richly

What! You've already seen them, Bellamy?

Bellamy

Oh—yes—have I seen them! I just left them. Mrs. Touchwood is in a horrible rage with you.

Richly

Against me?

Bellamy

Against you. "Oh, what," she said, "Mr. Richly has broken his word to us. Who would've believed it. My daughter is beside herself."

Richly

What wrong can it do her daughter?

Bellamy

That's what I told her. But what woman in a rage listens to reason? She doesn't believe for a minute that your son has already married a girl from Oxford. She thinks you decided you could make a better match.

Richly

This is awful. How can she imagine I would do such a thing?

Bellamy

She's out of her head. She rolls her eyes—she doesn't recognize anybody. She took me by the throat, and I had quite a time freeing myself from her claws.

Richly

And her husband?

Bellamy

Oh, as for Mr. Touchwood, I found him moderation itself. He only hit me twice.

Richly

You astonish me, Bellamy. How can they act so wild? You certainly cannot have explained all the circumstances.

Bellamy

I beg pardon, sir. I told them that your son had already celebrated his nuptials before the marriage ceremony, and that you consented only to avoid a lawsuit.

Richly

And that didn't calm them?

Bellamy

Oh, it calmed them. They became murderously calm. If you'll take my advice, you'll return to Oxford as fast as you can.

Richly

No, Bellamy, I wish to see them and explain things to them.

Bellamy

I'm not going to let you do it. I won't permit you to enter and be mutilated. If you absolutely insist on speaking to them, wait at least until they've had time to cool off.

Richly

That makes sense.

Bellamy

Put off your visit until tomorrow. They will be in a better frame of mind to receive you.

Richly

Right—they'll be less violent. Let's go—I am going to take your advice.

Bellamy

No, sir, do what you please. You are the master.

Richly

No, no—come, Bellamy. I will see them tomorrow.

(Exit Richly.)

Bellamy

I'll be right along. (low) Right after I see Bendish. We are at the very crisis of all our problems. I have a little scruple on the subject of the dowry. It irritates me to share with Bendish. After all, Angelica was supposed to marry my master—so why should Bendish have any of it? How can I cheat Bendish out of it? Suppose I convince him to spend the night with Angelica? A wife for one night only—he's attracted to her, and he's nutty enough to follow my advice. While he's amusing himself, I will be off with what really counts—the money. But no—it's a bad idea. No use getting in a brouhaha with someone as sly as myself. Someday he'd have his revenge. Besides, it would be against the law—the law of thieves. Our laws are more exacting than those of honest men.— Here comes Touchwood, going to see his solicitor.

(Enter Mr. Touchwood, accompanied by Lucy.)

Bellamy (leaving)

What a satisfaction, to have gotten Mr. Richly out of the way.

(Exit Bellamy.)

Lucy

And I repeat, sir, Worthy is an honest man, and you ought—

Mr. Touchwood

You are not too clever, Lucy. I know you're in Worthy's interest, and I'm angry with you for having invented this pretended marriage to divide me from Richly.

Lucy

What! Sir, do you imagine that I—?

Mr. Touchwood

No, Lucy. I don't imagine. I'm easy to deceive. I'm the easiest fellow in the world. Go, Lucy. Tell Worthy that he will never marry my daughter—and he can tell his creditors that, too.

Lucy

Listen, what is all this about? There's something going on that's beyond me.

(Exit Mr. Touchwood and enter Worthy from a different direction.)

Worthy

Despite what Bendish told me, I can't wait quietly to see how his trick will work. After all, he didn't explain why it's so important that I stay away. How my being here will spoil things, I can't figure out.

Lucy

Ah, sir.

Worthy

Well, Lucy?

Lucy

You've been awfully slow. Where's that letter?

Worthy (taking the letter from his pocket and showing it to her)

Here it is. But it will be useless to us now. Tell me, Lucy, how's the game going?

Lucy

What game?

Worthy

The game that Bendish has devised.

Lucy

Bendish—who the devil is Bendish?

Worthy

Why—my valet.

Lucy

I don't know him.

Worthy

This is pushing the dissimulation too far, Lucy. Bendish told me you were in on it.

Lucy

Sir, I don't know what you're talking about.

Worthy

Oh, no. This is too much. I lose patience. I am in despair.

(Enter Mrs. Touchwood and Angelica.)

Mrs. Touchwood

Well, I'm glad to find you, Worthy. Really! A nice young man like you, to forge letters.

Worthy

Forge? Me? Who can have told you such a lie?

Lucy

Oh, ma'am, Mr. Worthy isn't a forger. He's deceived in this affair. (seeing Mr. Touchwood) But, here is Mr. Touchwood, returning with Old Richly. Now we're going to find out the truth.

(Enter Mr. Touchwood and Richly.)

Mr. Touchwood

There's some kind of skullduggery involved here, Mr. Richly.

Richly

We've got to get to the bottom of it!

Mr. Touchwood (to his wife)

Madame, I've just met Mr. Richly while going to my solicitor. He comes, he says to London, to withdraw his promise. Young Richly is actually married.

Angelica

What do I hear?

Richly

Unfortunately, it's true, Madame—and when you know all the circumstances, you will forgive—

Mr. Touchwood (to his wife)

Mr. Richly was forced to consent, but what I don't understand is that he swears his son is still at Oxford.

Richly

Positively.

Mrs. Touchwood

Well, we've got a young rascal here who says he's your son.

Richly

An imposter!

Mr. Touchwood

And Bellamy, the same valet who was here with you two weeks ago, calls him his master—

Richly

Bellamy, you say? Ah! The gallows-bird! Now I understand why he prevented me from seeing you. He told me you were both in an uncontrollable rage with me, and that he was mistreated here.

Mrs. Touchwood

The liar!

Lucy

I'm beginning to see the light.

Worthy

So, the little traitor is playing games with me!

Mr. Touchwood (seeing Bellamy and Bendish)

We're going to find out soon enough. Here they both come.

(Enter Bellamy and Bendish.)

Bendish

Well! Mr. Touchwood, everything is in readiness—our marriage— (seeing Richly and Worthy) Ouf! What do I see?

Bellamy

Yipes, all is discovered. Run for it!

(Bellamy and Bendish run, but Worthy catches them both.)

Worthy

Oh, no, you don't escape, you pirates, and you will be punished as you deserve.

(Mr. Touchwood and Richly grab Bellamy.)

Mr. Touchwood

Ah! Ah! We've got you, you cheats.

Richly (to Bellamy)

Tell us, who is the scalawag you've been passing off as my son?

Worthy

It's my valet—Bendish.

Mrs. Touchwood

A valet! By the lord! A valet!

Worthy

A false creature, who made me think he was in my interests, only to deceive me, using the dirtiest of dirty tricks.

Bendish

Easy, sir, easy. Don't judge simply by appearances.

Richly

And you, asshole—what did you do with the money I gave you?

Bellamy

Gone, sir, gone—but if you please, don't condemn people without giving them a chance to speak.

Richly

What! You pretend you're not a world-class cheat?

Bellamy (crying)

I am a cheat! Very well, see the results of serving you too loyally.

Worthy (to Bendish)

You don't agree either, that you're a cheat and a swindler?

Bendish

Cheat! Swindler! What the devil, sir, you use words that I can't agree with at all.

Worthy

We're wrong to suspect you of disloyalty—right, traitors?

Mr. Touchwood

What have you to say to justify yourselves, wretches?

Bellamy

Wait, Bendish is going to explain everything.

Bendish

In two words, Bellamy will clear up the whole thing.

Bellamy

Say something, Bendish. Make them see we are innocent.

Bendish

Say something yourself, Bellamy. You will soon straighten them out.

Bellamy

No, no—you are better at disentangling things.

Bendish

Well, I'm going to explain everything just as it is. I took the name Richly in order to prejudice Mr. and Mrs. Touchwood against him because of my ridiculous behavior. Unfortunately, my manners, which were utterly deplorable, were somehow overlooked, and to tell the truth, found agreeable. That's really not my fault.

Richly

Now, if we hadn't stopped you, you'd have gone through with the game, and actually married my daughter—right?

Bendish

No, sir. We were coming here to tell you everything. Ask Bellamy.

Worthy

Not good enough! While Richly was married, there was no need to impersonate him.

Bendish (falling on his knees)

To tell the truth, gentlemen, while we are not quite innocent, be gracious enough to pardon us. We implore you.

Bellamy

Yes, we ask your clemency.

Bendish

Frankly, the dowry tempted us. We're used to cheating people. Forgive us. It was merely a matter of habit getting the best of us.

Mr. Touchwood

No, no. Your audacity has to be punished.

Bellamy

Oh, sir. We beg you, by the beautiful eyes of Mrs. Touchwood.

Bendish

By the tenderness you should feel for everyone—because you have such a charming wife and daughter.

Mrs. Touchwood

There pretty fellows awake my pity. I don't know why, but I like them. Pardon them.

Lucy

What smooth, clever cheats they are.

Richly

You're very lucky, gallows-birds, that Mrs. Touchwood intercedes for you.

Mr. Touchwood

I really want to punish you for the good of society—but since my wife will have it so—forget the past. So today, I give my daughter to Worthy. As for you two, I pardon you, and if you will promise to improve in the future, I will make your fortune.

Bendish

Oh, sir, we promise you, we'll reform.

Bellamy

Yes, sir. First thing. We are mortified not to succeed in our little scheme. So disgraced that we will renounce all cheating forever.

Mr. Touchwood

That's the spirit. But, it's necessary to insure your good behavior. I'll set you up in business.

Bellamy

Thank you, sir, with all my heart.

Bendish

I'll never forget you.

Mr. Touchwood

As for you, Bendish, I'm going to marry you to the daughter of a friend of mine, a rich bureaucrat.

Bendish

I will try to merit what you have done for me.

Mr. Touchwood

Let's not stay outside any longer. Come on in. I hope that Mr. Richly will honor us with his presence at my daughter's wedding.

Richly

I am going to dance with Mrs. Townly.

THE **CURTAIN** BEGINS TO FALL SLOWLY, THEN STOPS, HESITATES, AND GOES UP SLIGHTLY[1]

(All go into the house. The curtain is about to go down, and hesitates as Angelica enters, weeping, followed by Lucy.)

Angelica

Oh, Lucy, since Bendish has disclosed his passion for me, I feel as if—I feel as if—I feel if I marry Worthy I'll never be happy in my life.

Lucy

Miss Touchwood! What are you saying? You can't be in love with a valet?

Angelica

I can. I am. Woe is me. Help me, Lucy. What should I do? Tell

---
1. Lesage'S play ends here. I could not resist adding the remaining speeches when Angelica reenters until the final curtain. FJM

me, I beg you.

Lucy

The only thing I can think of is to talk to your mother. Like mother, like daughter.

CURTAIN

THE FORFEITURE
BY CHARLES DUFRESNY

CAST OF CHARACTERS

GERONTE, father of Isabelle

ISABELLE, lover of Valere

BELISE, Valere's older aunt

ARAMINTE, her younger sister

VALERE, nephew of Belise and Araminte

FRONTIN, Valere's valet

A LACKEY

Four men, three women

THE PLAY

Enter Isabelle and Valere from opposite directions without seeing each other.

VALERE:

What! Unable to reason with my two aunts!

ISABELLE:

I can never return. What extravagants!

VALERE:

Yes, the more I think of it, the less I see of a way out.

ISABELLE:

To have such revolting procedures for a nephew.

VALERE:

We shall get nothing out of it.

ISABELLE:

Oh Gods!

VALERE:

Cruel Aunts. For more than ten years always new injustices.

ISABELLE:

(seeing each other) What unpleasantness— But—

VALERE:

What cruelty! To be desolated side by side without finding any way to placate these crazies.

ISABELLE:

My father has spoken sharply to them and is going to threaten them again, separately. For each stays in her own apartment.

VALERE:

Yes, from the little I see, the two avoid each other, speak only a few words in passing, and leave each other. As for me, when I am speaking to them, they turn their backs. Their hardness towards me appears on every occasion.

ISABELLE:

Their hardness towards you condemns them. Ah, Valere, they push their ill natures too far. To not love you!

VALERE:

I hoped that through you, my two aunts would do something for us, and that having seen you, adorable Isabelle, they could be counted on.

ISABELLE:

Their barbarity is such that they speak of you with aversion.

VALERE:

What unpleasant spirits not to approve my tender passion.

ISABELLE:

To be capable of hating Valere. Their evil hearts make me tremble. I despair over it.

VALERE:

Your father is still going to press them. Thus we may still hope. He's going to meet us here.

ISABELLE:

Yes, give us at least a moment of hope. But I am indignant when I think of their latest remarks.

VALERE:

You should count on them for they showed you a hundred signs of friendship yesterday.

ISABELLE:

It's from that that I see they have scorned me. For only in embracing did they refuse me. The Prude scorned me with her haughty airs, took a soft tone mixed with disdain, affected caresses and vapid joking. You die in flattery.

"My tenderness for you," she told me very loudly, "makes

me not want you to marry so soon. That is to say, to give to a nephew who presses me some wealth to satisfy a mad passion; no, I would become your accomplice in authorizing it." And a hundred like remarks, in a somewhat pleasant tone, made against marriage. "Be like us, a forfeiture makes you wise. Imitate our strength of character. One refusal will keep you at least from any forfeiture."

VALERE:

What stupid remarks. Always the same rubric. But nothing comes from their gothic spirit. Without worldliness, visiting no one except her sister who is less hard than she is, but crazier from misfortune.

ISABELLE:

I am a little less furious with Araminte. For a few moments I thought I'd won her over. But her character is subject to change. Agitating itself with several passions at the same time, in her burning and turbulent vivacity. Here's what was told me by this aunt: "I rave from time to time, but I have some sentiments. I love love, but I hate lovers. Abhor them, too. I intend it, I order it. Without cease I promise but I never give, I hate my nephew a lot but I love you a great deal." From this balderdash I still conclude that she will do more for you than her sister.— My father's coming.

VALERE:

I am going to learn my fate.

ISABELLE:

I tremble. Oh, I see him overwhelmed with chagrin.

VALERE:

His approach seizes me. My misfortune is certain.

(Enter Geronte)

GERONTE:

You perceive by observing my sadness that I have received only a refusal. My goodness, my fondness spoke loudly for you on this occasion. Take your leave, daughter.

ISABELLE:

Must we part?

GERONTE:

Yes, daughter.

VALERE:

What can I think?

ISABELLE:

Oh. What a blow to Valere.

GERONTE:

Your aunts have made this separation imperative.

VALERE:

What, charming Isabelle, I mustn't see you anymore? What, sir, do you wish to put me in despair? You are going to tear me from

Isabelle!

GERONTE:

Yes, Valere.

VALERE:

Ah, at least beg your father to stay in Paris several more days.

ISABELLE:

No, Valere.

VALERE:

Oh, sir.

GERONTE:

Useless words.

VALERE:

Oh, if it is your wish, adorable Isabelle.

GERONTE:

I don't wish it, but through care of her. She wishes that which it is her duty to wish. To return to the country immediately without seeing you any further.

VALERE:

And you consent to this?

ISABELLE:

It's better so, Valere. I gave you my heart by order of my father. I obeyed him. He now intends, wisely, that I separate from you. It must be admitted frankly that I am not sure of a like obedience. But I am going.

VALERE:

What, sir, deny me all hope?

GERONTE:

Better to give you no hope when I have none. You hoped to get 40,000 écus restitution from your aunts. I tell you again, these two extravagants intend to keep that forfeiture, saying you cannot get it from us unless one of us marries. They're both over fifty. It's a joke to believe that will happen. I need money. My wealth is perishing. Expenses are ruining me. So, as a wise man, I ought to go back to the country and contract a marriage that will get me out of this financial trouble.

VALERE:

True, but—

GERONTE:

Let's break it off, then. It's with great shame, but tomorrow we part, that's certain.

ISABELLE:

Oh, Valere; if I'm under orders from my father, be sure that in parting—

GERONTE:

(taking Isabelle by the arm) Let's shorten the goodbyes. When one must leave, the shortest is the best.

(Exit Isabelle and Geronte)

VALERE:

I am in despair. This parting kills me.

(Enter Frontin dressed as a cavalier, passing before Valere who is in despair)

FRONTIN:

Sir.

VALERE:

What is it then?

FRONTIN:

It's Fortune greeting you.

VALERE:

What do I see?

FRONTIN:

You see Frontin who was wearing livery this morning.

VALERE:

What are you talking about? Why are you dressed this way?

FRONTIN:

You will never guess, I bet.

VALERE:

Whose clothes are you wearing? It's one of mine, I believe.

FRONTIN:

Could well be, 'cause it's none of mine.

VALERE:

And my wig.

FRONTIN:

Good. Have I bought it. I found this under my hand, quite ready. And your most handsome lace, and largest jewel.

VALERE:

I've seen you do crazy things before, but nothing touching such insolence.

FRONTIN:

It's come right on time, sir, this opulence.

VALERE:

Scoundrel, you've picked a bad time to joke.

FRONTIN:

I picked my time just right, I dare to boast. To know how to manage times for a master.

VALERE:

To dare appear like this!

FRONTIN:

Sir, till now, I've been careful to conceal my scoundrel-like and insolent traits. That's why you hired me! Only working first on my own affairs, I have taken care to hide my traits with all necessary skill. You would have prevented me from acting as I have done. To deceive cleverly is virtue in a valet. You will have it that it's a vice in a master. I must tell you you are scrupulous to a fault. What I have done for you was done unknown to you.

VALERE:

What have you done for me?

FRONTIN:

It's a mere nothing. I'm working on marrying you to Isabelle.

VALERE:

Frontin, my dear Frontin. You are working for me. In what way? How? Explain quickly!

FRONTIN:

Let me explain first how I am to be rewarded. That's how I get to be zealous. If I get your Isabelle for you—

VALERE:

Well?

FRONTIN:

Lace, clothes, diamond: I won't return them. If the outfit is too short, too long, for better or for worse—I get it. As for the diamond, it's made for me.

VALERE:

I will give you all.

FRONTIN:

Listen to my story. With a little money, this brilliant outfit and finding a place at a card table and some winning cards, and ogling some of the old girls playing, with one especially, I got in deep. She has a sterile wit but babbles constantly. Always joking, she is more crazy than funny. Do you recognize her, sir? She's your aunt.

VALERE:

It's herself. Well, you are telling me you won money from my aunt at cards?

FRONTIN:

A little. But I won more of her heart. She adores me.

VALERE:

She loves you!

FRONTIN:

Yes, sir. And better yet, she wants to marry me.

VALERE:

Great.

FRONTIN:

Your valet Frontin could become your uncle or uncle-in-law tomorrow.

VALERE:

What! Seriously?

FRONTIN:

The lady is serious. I have the looks to make an old woman amorous.

FRONTIN:

Without doubt. But still, to marry you must know the man.

FRONTIN:

She knows me extremely well. A month of card-playing causes you to know a chap extremely well. Saying I'm from a land between Paris and Rome, I took a name; a name half-known there. Taking in those that have never been there.

VALERE:

What name?

FRONTIN:

The Chevalier de Cique. A noble name. She believes I'm from an ancient family.

VALERE:

I cannot get over my astonishment.

FRONTIN:

Good! But that's nothing yet; I have done even more.

VALERE:

What?

FRONTIN:

Seeing that fortune gave me one aunt, still there remained another—

VALERE:

Well?

FRONTIN:

A difficult, astonishing, a hazardous plan. In the same house I see them both. It's true, I know that since she became amorous, Araminte is ashamed, fearful of her sister. For more security against the other, I take a different name, character, arms, clothes. From a grave Senechal, I adopt the character, a composed air, grave tone, cold face, saying nothing like she does in a sententious tone, and like her a fastidious censor of marriage. My name as Senechal is Groux. I present myself. Similarity of character charms the prudish aunt. And in a word, sir, I succeeded.

VALERE:

What's this? My other aunt?

FRONTIN:

She's going to marry me, also.

VALERE:

Singular fact. But from their benevolence how do you propose to extract—?

FRONTIN:

From their extravagance I believe we will get some money for a forfeiture. But tell me, how was their double forfeiture written?

VALERE:

Here's how. You know their cruel tricks. I have been unable to get any restitution from them. The only thing they would agree to was that if they should marry, in order that I would not lose my claim to the inheritance, they would each give me 100,000 francs. However, they have sworn never to marry, and they've kept their oaths constantly so far. These forfeitures are under seal.

FRONTIN:

Then that is how I'll get the money. But I intend— Ah good, it's a lackey of mine.

(Enter Lackey)

LACKEY:

Time passes, sir. To the notary and explain. Disguise yourself. All will be lost. (Frontin puts on a brown coat and a black wig)

FRONTIN:

It's necessary that I first be Senechal Groux. Wait for me upstairs at Aunt Araminte's. She's getting ready to leave. There I can go without fear and instruct you in everything.

VALERE:

I am going there.

FRONTIN:

I will rejoin you.

(Exit Valere)

FRONTIN:

(to Lackey) I thought I'd have two days' time at least. But both of them taking the money to the notary are going to discover the trick. We'll have to speed up the affair.

(Exit Lackey, enter Belise)

FRONTIN:

Good. The prude is leaving. By having imitated trait for trait her insipidity, her cold gravity, I pleased her. There's no other way to please this foolish woman except by echoing her vapid whims.— Madame.

BELISE:

Ah, Senechal. What! You are here. I see you again.

FRONTIN:

You see? As for me, I see you again, too.

BELISE:

Once more I see the happiness of an unfeeling woman.

FRONTIN:

I see again the happiness of a fireproof man.

BELISE:

Who looks with frigidity on the most charming of men.

FRONTIN:

Who views with disdain the most loveable object.

BELISE:

Preceded by terror, considering my love. I am astonished to see this extreme change you've wrought in me in less than two weeks.

FRONTIN:

I see with a kind of horror that you have effected a metamorphosis in me.

BELISE:

Both of us, at the same time, think the same thing?

FRONTIN:

The same thing, and always sympathy between us.

BELISE:

What a coincidence! Oh, heaven! To take you for a spouse. That makes me tremble.

FRONTIN:

I quiver, Madame, on account of the step I am going to take, by taking you for my wife.

BELISE:

I, who by my example have kept my sister in the vow she made to guard her heart. She respected me as the most perfect. I must blush before my little sister.

FRONTIN:

I who to my elders reprimanded passions, forcing even my sisters to celibacy, I who in history to distinguish my name would have gloried in the title of extinguisher of my race—

BELISE:

I who abhorred even the name of marriage and would have become famous for it.

FRONTIN:

I, Senechal Groux, caustic philosopher who jested at suitors, insulted them, apostrophized them.

BELISE:

I called marriage a myth, a stumbling block.

FRONTIN:

The prison of desires, the coffin of the living.

BELISE:

(tenderly) The abyss. Now see what an unfeeling fondness—

FRONTIN:

Towards the abyss, a slope—

BELISE:

Yes, sweet—

FRONTIN:

Imperceptible—

BELISE:

Leads me to the brink—

FRONTIN:

The foot slips and here I am.

BELISE:

Here I am. But at least the world agrees I have chosen you from taste, from wisdom.

FRONTIN:

Our marriage is the wisest type.

BELISE:

But all my embarrassment is, that by marrying, I must—here's the trouble—I must pay this forfeiture. What to do? This forfeiture note that I gave to Valere. That crazy sister of mine invented the forfeiture. We made two promissory notes to this cursed nephew. All falls on me, since I am marrying, so I will have to pay up all by myself, and I'm going to have to put up with all kinds of jesting from her. Blush to death.

FRONTIN:

While our love remains secret, compose yourself and retrieve your promissory notes from Valere.

BELISE:

That's my intention. I am going to my notary to take some money to my nephew. Without a doubt he will instantly return my promissory note to me. But if my sister should learn of it, oh, my heart palpitates. From reason and from shame, I avoid her carefully. After seeing you, I dare not see her.

(Exit Belise)

FRONTIN:

We shall get to tap that money she's going to receive.

(Enter Lackey)

LACKEY:

Sir, change clothes or hide yourself quickly. Araminte has returned.

FRONTIN:

I ought to avoid her. But no. Let's pull it off! I am going to wait for her here. Time presses. Wait, take this wig. By knotting it this way, I will have the most comic look. Playful, negligent. It's the Chevalier Cique. To charm a madwoman you have to rave.

(Exit Lackey, enter Araminte)

ARAMINTE (assuming all passions, one after another)

I run in thoughtless. They've just been plotting against me. I tremble; I still have a hundred things to say to you. And jests. First, I am going to make you laugh. But no. The serious is more pressing. My sister, seeing me there, passed by proudly. I was trembling. It's of this we will speak first. Let's begin by you admiring my conduct, the softness and complacency with which I hide my shame. Now, in secret, I hoped, but I fear. At the same time I sense an infinite joy. You are going to deliver me from the tyranny of my sister. And the more I hate that nephew, the more I am going to settle everything for you on that score. But tell me first: what part should I take? Speak slowly, for I love to hear you. When you breathe, I listen. Speak of your love and let me reply. Speak.

FRONTIN:

If I am silent, it's because the crowd of my passions is rolling in me, as in you, and are preventing me from speaking. For in vivacity, I dare equal you. But my love has reduced me to silence. I was unable to say a word, 'cause you were speaking.

ARAMINTE:

You are all wit, although you are quiet. For you, your manners, your looks, all speak loudly. All speak your heart, my dear Chevalier de Cique!

FRONTIN:

Everything in you is beautiful. All of me loves you. Everything in me, everything in you, a charming agreement that demands marriage.

ARAMINTE:

It's true. But I fear this forfeiture which preoccupies me. And I fear still more this severe sister who believes that, alas, it is a crime to have a heart; she made me take a vow of indifference when I would have broken it in my childhood. That is to say, from the age when my discernment had been able to distinguish you, to choose you for my lover. Yes, my dear Chevalier, yes, I repeat it to you, I love you, I love you too late. I regret without cease the years I have spent without knowing you.

FRONTIN:

I'm only twenty-five, but I would have come into the world twenty years sooner to know you. Yes, time is dear to us, as it ought to be. Let us see quickly. Let's decide. Have you resolved?

ARAMINTE:

I've looked, looked again, decided, determined, concluded. Ought I to be in fear of this savage sister who hates marriage for herself and for me? You will be my husband from tomorrow, from this evening.

FRONTIN:

But to the essential. You must be able, before declaring our business to your sister, to get rid of those promissory notes to Valere. Reach an agreement with him. Is your money ready?

ARAMINTE:

Yes, I've withdrawn everything. It is in my interest this forfeiture be taken care of, alas, before my sister learns of my marriage. I am prudent and wise.

FRONTIN:

Haste! I am going to see my illustrious relatives to tell them the role I am taking.

(Exit Frontin)

ARAMINTE:

Let's quickly send a lackey to Valere. But what do I see! My sister returning from the notary. She's going to be irritated about the money I've taken out. He's just informed her.

(Enter Belise. They don't speak to each other at first.)

BELISE:

Yes, my sister is going to see the Notary. She's going to guess the mystery.

ARAMINTE:

I see she's upset. Oh, I hear her rage. Where shall I tell her I intend to place the money?

BELISE:

Ah, I see that she knows it. What it will cost me to say that this money is for my marriage?

ARAMINTE:

Sooner or later my sister must confide in me.

BELISE:

I tremble. Dare I make her my full confidante? Let's try. Let's talk to her.

ARAMINTE:

(aloud) Sister.

BELISE:

(aloud) Sister, I think— (aside) Oh, fear seizes me!

ARAMINTE:

(aside) Shame smothers my voice.

BELISE: (aloud)

To put money when the law—

ARAMINTE:

When one disposes of joint funds by oneself—

BELISE:

One ought to warn of taking it, but one dares not—

ARAMINTE:

One ought to confide in her sister.

BELISE:

Yes, of course—

ARAMINTE:

One ought—

BELISE:

One is afraid—

ARAMINTE:

It's I.—

BELISE:

I admit it—

ARAMINTE:

I was wrong.

BELISE:

One ought to ask pardon—

ARAMINTE:

A fault so huge—

BELISE:

Yes, when one is promised—

ARAMINTE:

Sister, I ask your pardon—

BELISE:

Pardon, sister—

ARAMINTE:

Pardon.

BELISE:

Pardon.

ARAMINTE:

What? We are asking each other for pardon?

BELISE:

But truly, you ask me. What is your offense then?

ARAMINTE:

I believe it was you who asked first. What have you done to me?

BELISE:

But you, too, sister?

ARAMINTE:

Tell me your secrets.

BELISE:

Open your heart to me.

ARAMINTE:

Oh, well. You will doubtless have learned from the notary that I have taken this money.

BELISE:

Your business. You are right to take your wealth. For each can dispose of hers as she pleases.

ARAMINTE:

To place it elsewhere, I thought I had the right to take it.

BELISE:

You don't owe me any accounting. I have taken mine as well.

ARAMINTE:

So much the better, sister, so much the better. On that account I calm my curiosity.

BELISE:

You have good sense. You are not being irritating.

ARAMINTE:

One is liberal with you because you are charming.

BELISE:

Alas, I never irritated you about anything. Except about marriage, and that was for your good. If boredom at being a maiden made you do it, I would be compassionate, like a tender sister—for a weakness.

ARAMINTE:

You will never have such a weakness. If you come to that—and the wisest have—far from condemning you, I would be complaisant about it.

BELISE:

Ah, be sure of my condescension.

ARAMINTE:

Sometimes we must be humane to each other.

BELISE:

Alas, I, in getting married would authorize you to do so, without wishing you ill for it.

ARAMINTE:

Yes, marry quickly, yes. I would be ravished, for then I could—

BELISE:

What? Why?

ARAMINTE:

But, sister—

BELISE:

Could you have been capable of letting your heart be surprised?

ARAMINTE:

And you?

BELISE:

But you—

ARAMINTE:

But you—

BELISE:

Eh!

ARAMINTE:

But yes.

BELISE:

Me, too.

ARAMINTE:

Embrace me, sis.

BELISE:

Sis, how I love you. Yes, we are truly sisters today.

ARAMINTE:

You know, good hearts are always made for love. You would have stayed a maid. What folly!

BELISE:

Like you, I wonder how we made that imprudent vow thirty years ago.

ARAMINTE:

The one you love, you have freely. Without doubt, dear sister, wise as you are, you have meditated over the choice that you've made.

BELISE:

You whose taste is so fine, so exquisite, undoubtedly you made your choice with discernment.

ARAMINTE:

Lively, playful, humorous. He's an amiable young man.

BELISE:

The one that I love is young and yet respectable; wise, grave, self-possessed.

ARAMINTE:

Mine always has the air—

BELISE:

A solidity—

ARAMINTE:

Brilliant like a flash of lightning.

BELISE:

Who rarely speaks but with weight and measure.

ARAMINTE:

Mine talks ceaselessly and about everything. But always well.

BELISE:

Like you, I see you and I have chosen our spouses according to our characters.

ARAMINTE:

It's prudent.

BELISE:

It's wisdom. Mine has wealth, birth, esteem. He's the Senechal Groux.

ARAMINTE:

That's a man who is known. Like you, I have found a noble spouse. But of ancient nobility. A distinguished man. He's the Chevalier Cique.

BELISE:

They speak well of him. Your vote, sister, and the voice of the people honor him.

ARAMINTE:

The public ought to praise us for our choices, But, in other respects, we've had strange obstacles. This forfeiture, for example—

BELISE:

Yes, this forfeit, right.

ARAMINTE:

Our promissory notes.

BELISE:

Our promissory notes.

ARAMINTE:

We've suffered a great wrong. To promise this nephew a hundred thousand francs each.

BELISE:

I have just refused this importunate demand and I believe he's unaware of our plans. For a little money he will return our notes to us.

ARAMINTE:

But to discharge them, what trick can we employ?

(Enter Geronte, Valere, Isabelle)

VALERE:

(to Geronte) Take advantage of the opportunity. Better not wait. They are pushing their explanation a long way. (aloud) Isabelle didn't leave my aunts happily. And I've learned some good news.

GERONTE:

I come to rejoice for the sake of Isabelle's love.

ISABELLE:

I come with all my heart to congratulate you, and I saw immediately it was in joking that you always declaimed against marriage, for you yourselves—

ARAMINTE:

We ourselves—

BELISE:

Ah, sis, what language—

VALERE:

You are both going to get married.

ARAMINTE:

(low) So as not to pay out, sister, we must deny it.

BELISE:

The rumor is false.

ARAMINTE:

Very false.

VALERE:

Aunties, I believe it's true.

BELISE:

What? You takes us for some extravagants? Us, marry! Us!

ARAMINTE:

We, no, no. It's no longer time.

BELISE:

No, don't think it. I am past forty.

VALERE:

You're not.

ARAMINTE:

And I am more than fifty.

VALERE:

No.

BELISE:

We are—

ISABELLE:

No.

ARAMINTE:

The dispute is funny. I believe we know our age better than you. He's joking. And, sister, the notes he has from us are worthless. Worth nothing. It's a vain hope.

BELISE:

They are worth nothing. But, sister, Isabelle and Valere have a tender feeling for each other. Their legitimate flames make me pity them. Can they, like we, hate marriage? No. We must do something to their advantage. They move me.

ARAMINTE:

Yes, we are moved.

VALERE:

You will be moved. Your notes will be fine.

BELISE:

Let's not joke further. We will give Valere 10,000 écus in all.

ARAMINTE:

Yes. That's what we must do.

VALERE:

No, no. We will wait for it all.

BELISE:

Huh?

ISABELLE:

Nothing presses us.

ARAMINTE:

Take advantage of the opportunity.

VALERE:

We will wait for you.

ARAMINTE:

Because I am generous: fifty thousand franks.

BELISE:

That's too much. But I will equal it from generosity.

VALERE:

Fifty thousand écus. We shall wait.

BELISE:

Oh, I won't keep more for you.

ARAMINTE:

My nephew, my nephew,

ISABELLE:

Manage them, Valere, because fifty thousand francs is enough for my father.

GERONTE:

Yes, that's enough.

ARAMINTE:

So as not to dispute further, give them.

BELISE:

Come then, we will execute—

ARAMINTE:

I have on me what I got from the notary.

BELISE:

He has given me some to end this business.

VALERE:

Let's see if by chance I don't have your promissory notes. Yes, truly, I believe they are here.

GERONTE:

The business seems to me easy to finish.

VALERE:

Let's see.

BELISE:

This is my note.

ARAMINTE:

Here's my signature.

BELISE:

Forty thousand francs on my banker and ten.

ARAMINTE:

Thirty thousand in bills of exchange plus fourteen and six.

VALERE:

What happiness.

ISABELLE:

I breathe.

VALERE:

With great pleasure I tear up your forfeitures.

(Enter Frontin with a cape, a short wig and a cap like Pasquin)

FRONTIN:

Our lovers are satisfied. We must amuse them.

ARAMINTE:

Oh, it's you, Chevalier. Why are you dressed like that?

BELISE:

Oh. It's the Senechal. What is this mystery? Why aren't you wearing your usual clothes?

FRONTIN:

Here I am only a servant-chevalier.

ARAMINTE:

He's playful.

BELISE:

But Senechal—

FRONTIN:

Although Senechal, I often wear livery.

BELISE:

Have you gone mad?

ARAMINTE:

Drunk on pleasures, my sister sees in you her lover, the Senechal, dear Chevalier.

BELISE:

Sister we are misunderstanding each other. He's the Senechal Groux.

ARAMINTE:

But I think you are dreaming. He's my Chevalier Cique.

FRONTIN:

Yes, from complacency to please the younger, I am playful, lively, and to please the elder, stern. But unable to be two except in appearance, I must admit that Frontin is neither Cique nor Groux.

BELISE:

What?

ARAMINTE:

How's that?

VALERE:

It's Frontin himself.

BELISE:

Where are we?

VALERE:

A scoundrel of a valet to pretend to be such a person.

ARAMINTE:

A valet?

BELISE:

A valet.

GERONTE:

The wisest thing would be to ask us about this matter in private.

ISABELLE:

Pardon the nephew for the valet's sake.

BELISE:

Oh, sister.

ARAMINTE:

Oh, sis, let's hide our shame from them.

(Exit Araminte and Belise)

VALERE:

The fear they have of making the subject of a fine story, perhaps, may make them less unjust to me.

FRONTIN:

In comic moral, it is, I believe, permitted, for Frontin to punish the aunts' avarice and to make fun of these broken-down lovers.

CURTAIN

ABOUT THE EDITOR

Frank J. Morlock has written and translated many plays since retiring from the legal profession in 1992. His translations have also appeared on Project Gutenberg, the Alexandre Dumas Père web page, Literature in the Age of Napoléon, Infinite Artistries.com, and Munsey's (formerly Blackmask). In 2006 he received an award from the North American Jules Verne Society for his translations of Verne's plays. He lives and works in México.

www.ingramcontent.com/pod-product-compliance
Lightning Source LLC
LaVergne TN
LVHW041617070426
835507LV00008B/289